MC

the pilgrimage

50 places to surf before you die

the pilgrimage

50 places to surf before you die

edited by sean doherty

VIKING
an imprint of
PENGUIN BOOKS

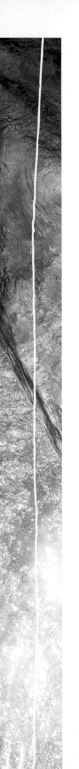

contents

introduction

The 50 waves in this book are real pieces of work. Magic amalgams of rock, sand and saltwater, capable of everything a wave is capable of. Capable of delivering the greatest moment of a surfer's life. Capable of compelling a man to throw away life as he once knew it for a single wave. In the 100 years of the modern surfing era, these are the waves – by and large – that have captured the surfing imagination more than any other. They've been perpetuated in surfing folklore to the point where they've developed a life force of their own.

For the guys who surf these places daily, these waves take on human qualities: one day an old friend, the next a malignant shadow bristling with intent. But like humans they are also supremely fallible. Two-foot onshore Pipeline is as bad as two-foot onshore anywhere. Lagundri? It was completely flat when I spent my first week there. I've also been dragged screaming across the reef at Teahupoo, crying like a child, on a timid four-foot day. Driving over the headland and seeing one of these spots laid out before you for the first time, you may find it doesn't quite match up to the seductive promise held out by every embellished tale or glossy article you've encountered about the place. So much hype has been documented about these waves that the line in the sand between myth and reality has, in many cases, been washed away like a low-tide footprint. And therein lies the beauty of experiencing them for yourself.

Your life is full of choices. You can choose to go to the grave with more consumer products – more cars, more electric nose-hair trimmers – than your neighbour, or you can choose to spend the afterlife with the Cheshire grin of a man who's surfed some of the world's best waves on their all-time days. The better human beings I know all fall into the latter category. Many guys I know who've travelled extensively are lucky to possess two coins to rub together, but are spiritually rolling in the stuff.

What would you swap for a barrel at Pipeline? A plasma TV? A house deposit? If you're a true surfer, your first-born child should be nervous if you were asked this question. You're a long time dead and a short time in your surfing prime, my friend. Before the anchors of full-time employment, relationships and kids slow your ship, you owe it to yourself – to your surfing – to see them at close range, preferably from the inside looking out.

SEAN DOHERTY
June 2007

anchor point
morocco
ben mondy

When it comes to surfing pilgrimages, the journey to the fabled righthand peelers of Morocco's Anchor Point must be one of the most chronicled, travelled and celebrated. It has all the checklist points of a classic surf trip: epic waves; strange, dangerous and exotic culture clashes; the fleeing of the cold and normal into the realms of the hot and spicy. For Europeans, the mission to Morocco is as much a rite of passage as a trip to Indonesia for Aussies or the run down to Mexico for Americans. Simply, if you want to be a proper surfer, it's important – no, essential – that you make one of these journeys.

The first missions to Anchor Point started way back in the 1960s. Tahgazout, the village about 15 minutes walk from the break, became known as a counter-culture hangout. Hippies and surfers and drop-outs and drop-kicks and wasters and rock'n'roll stars and artists and God knows what else rediscovered a town that had warmth in winter, blue crystal waters, white sand, cheap, cheap, dope and, more importantly, sand-bottom points that reeled off for hundreds of metres.

The Rolling Stones jammed here, while Jimi Hendrix came within a hallucination of buying the neighbouring town, Essaouira. During the 70s the hippie movement died, and the celebrities moved on to the next depraved hotspot. What didn't go, though, were the waves, or the surfers who had found a source of mechanical tubes that ran right throughout the harsh European winter. Since then, Anchor Point and the waves nearby have become the last stop on an epic surf trip. In a cheap van with too many boards, too many surfers, and not enough money, the typical trip would start with the French beachies. Once sick of the cold, or the bread, it was then onwards through Spain and Portugal before crossing the Mediterranean onto Africa. Assuming you survived the seething myriad of scammers, you'd hammer down the long road to Taghazout.

Here, hopefully, you'd turn up to see a fresh groundswell running down the sandbank at Anchor Point. The sand would be packed and ordered from a month of swell, resulting in 500-metre rights peeling off in freight-train bursts and intermittent wide blue carve-me-please walls. You'd shell out a pittance for a small flat and once again, after packing into it way too many surfers and boards, would proceed to surf and smoke for months at a time, spending about 20 dollars a week.

Of course, times have changed, but that pilgrimage remains a European staple. Sure, other waves have been discovered in Morocco – some arguably of higher quality – and now you can get cheap flights from London to the capital,

Anchor Point and the waves nearby have become the last stop on an epic surf trip.

Agadir, which is only a 45-minute drive away, for the same price as a tank of fuel for the Kombi. But the allure is still there: the mix of French, Muslim and western culture; the towns of white-walled rectangular blocks; the cheap, amazing food. And, of course, the waves. Although they are sand-dependent and hardly ever empty, it is the quality of the sandbottomed break that makes this a special part of the surfing world.

anchor point facts

location   Just north of the capital, Agadir, on the south-central coast of Morocco.

getting there   Fly into Agadir, just a 45-minute drive away.

the perfect day   Six–eight feet, sunny and offshore. All the surrounding waves are firing and so the crowds are thin. And those who are surfing are too stoned to paddle anyway.

best months   October–April, the northern-hemisphere winter.

boards   Fish for the beachies, a couple of shortboards, and a semi-gun when it gets bigger, as a fair bit of water can move around.

essentials   All the necessary paperwork regarding insurance, travel plans and your finances. The customs officials are notorious. Also a 3/2 steamer, as despite the warm weather the water stays at about 17°C.

accommodation   In the town of Taghazout there is a wide range of very cheap apartment-style accommodation.

other waves   On their day the next two points north, Mysteries and Killers, are similar style rights that rival Anchor Point in quality and length.

angourie
australia
sean doherty

Angourie is one of the rare entries into this list that has withstood the ravages of its surfing notoriety. In fact, if anything, this world-famous righthand point break may in fact be more laid-back today than at any time in the past 20 millennia.

The flat, boulder-strewn headland, connected to the coast by a sandy isthmus, has been an important meeting place for the Yaegl people for generations. From here they could survey to the north, south and east, and it was they who named the place Angourie, which translated to 'the sound of the wind'. The only sounds that emanated from Angourie following white settlement, however, were those of coal-powered diggers chewing out bluestone from the neighbouring headland, to provide stone for the Clarence River breakwall at Yamba. When they dug into a freshwater spring and the pit flooded, it was abandoned, forming Angourie's famous Blue Pools, from where today you can look across the bay straight into the eye of the Angourie barrel.

While Angourie had been a meeting place for local Aborigines for thousands of years, come the 1970s a very different tribe was congregating here. As carloads of surfers fled both the city and gainful employment, Angourie became a metaphorical escape from the pressures of urban living. It's hardly surprising that the airbrushed green walls of the point became a studio for the filming of *Morning of the Earth*, a movie that encapsulated the country-soul generation more than any other.

It's still easy to see what attracted these urban refugees forty years ago. The waves, in the right conditions, can be awesome. The jump-off spot is out the back of the point, and while it's nowhere near as lethal as the Lennox jump-off just up the coast, it's still best to follow someone who knows what they're doing. The take-off spot is reasonably forgiving, although your thirty-odd new mates sitting out there with you are unlikely to be. Once the wave rounds the point and wraps into the bay, it throws big, barrelling sections interspersed with fast green walls custom-made for burying some rail. The wave has two faces, depending on the swell direction. Swells from the south wrap more gently around the point and are best described as fun. If, however, the swell is coming from the east or north, courtesy of a tropical cyclone, the swell will push back in on itself, much the same as Honolua Bay does, and the place can get heavy, handling eight to 10 feet of swell before closing out.

The blissed-out hippie days of having the point to yourself have, however, gone the same way as the single-fin. There may not be many locals in the Angourie area, but they can all surf the place in their sleep. Combined with a steady inflow of transient surfers, the drop-in factor out here on a good day is white-hot. When you mention Angourie to surfers around the world, the immediate image they have is of surfing legend and Angourie local Nat Young, his head looking like a blueberry muffin. Back in 2000, Young was involved in a fracas with another local surfer, the dust-up gaining international headlines and coining the term 'surf rage'.

If you grow up in Angourie, your career paths are somewhat limited – you'll be either a professional surfer or a fisherman. The current population is somewhere around 300, and it's unlikely to get any bigger. Bordered by national park, the village was recently declared Australia's third surfing reserve, ensuring its protection for future generations. There's never been a surfing contest held at Angourie, and there's not going to be one scheduled there any time soon.

angourie facts

location   Just south of Yamba on the far north coast of New South Wales.

getting there   Eight hours drive north of Sydney, or two hours south of the Gold Coast.

the perfect day   Four to six feet of easterly swell, with a south-west wind.

best months   February–September.

boards   Your normal shortboard, with something a little longer in case you encounter some serious swell.

essentials   A good set of wheels, some patience, a fishing rod.

accommodation   While Angourie has a few accommodation options, they are pretty exclusive and can be expensive. Your best bet is to try the nearby fishing town of Yamba, which has plenty of cheaper places.

other waves   Off the adjacent headland is the reef break known as Spookies, a heavier proposition than Angourie itself. There are good summer beachies on the southern side of the headland and, an hour in both directions, more waves than you could ever know what to do with.

arugam bay
sri lanka
sean doherty

Arugam Bay has been a pencil scratch on the hippie surf map since the 1970s, and it's not hard to imagine why – an ancient spiritual culture, an island oasis, and an endless, palm-fringed right. But while Bali today is largely unrecognisable as the one the first surfers visited 35 years ago, Sri Lanka's Arugam Bay has largely been frozen in time. The backdrop of jungle and rice paddies, single-laned potholed roads, temple ruins, fishing boats, tuk-tuks and elephants all retain the same exotic allure that seduced the first surfing refugees – not to mention the odd half-mile righthander. It's just the surfing clientele who've changed a bit these days.

The reason for this, sadly, is civil war. For 20 years the fighting that has ripped Sri Lanka apart and killed more than 60 000 people has occasionally rolled down the cheek of the teardrop island nation into the quiet southeastern corner. Some of the more hardcore travellers will recount close calls as Tamil Tigers skirmished with government forces while Arugam Bay pumped nearby.

Even though civil unrest continues in the north of the country today, you wouldn't know it if you were kicking stones and dodging roadside roosters up the main street of Arugam Bay. In fact, it's not the Tamil Tigers you should be worried about, but rather your taxi driver falling asleep on the eight-hour drive from the island's capital. The roads in

Sri Lanka are notorious death traps, and they, not civil war, are the biggest cause of death in the country today. But just when A-Bay was starting to re-establish itself on the maps of travelling surfers, the 2004 Boxing Day tsunami ripped through the area, levelling many of the flimsy lodgings that line the main road. After all they've been through, it's a wonder that today the only thing more blinding than the white-sand beach at midday is the smiles on the faces of the locals. And therein lies the charm of this place,

The wave at Arugam is long, forgiving, and as much fun as you could ever want. On a good day, the point can run anywhere up to 500 metres, long enough to scupper any plans of paddling back out and making the walk back up the beach a more enticing proposition, even if it is 35°C in the shade. The point breaks over a mix of sand and reef, and will occasionally barrel, even though it's more renowned for long, workable, fun walls. The place picks up more swell than any break in the region, and this, combined with the global notoriety of the wave, means it's pretty well always full of punters. The good news for the surfer who knows what he's doing is that a large chunk of this crowd is composed of clueless Euros. While the local guys surf the place well and are beginning to dominate the line-up (as they rightly should), your main competition for set waves might come from visiting Israeli surfers who here are earning a reputation for hassling that equals that of the Brazilians in Bali.

If solitude's your thing, there's an even longer point an hour's tuk-tuk ride back up the coast, in the town of Pottuvil, which you may need to surf to regain your sanity. The southeastern corner is also one of the most beautiful parts of the island, and if the surf goes flat there's plenty to see. The area is fringed by Lahugala and Yala national parks, and at Pottivul are the ruins of a 2000-year-old temple.

Conversely you could sit back in a bar on the point, drinking $1 beers and letting the day drift by. The living at A-Bay is cheap, the food is incredible, and the locals are among the friendliest people you'll find on the planet. But whether or not A-Bay is able to maintain its old-school charm under the onslaught of the surfing armies of the new millennium, we'll just have to wait and see.

arugam bay facts

location   Southeastern corner of Sri Lanka, 320 km from Colombo.

getting there   Fly into Colombo, and then negotiate a taxi for the roughly eight-hour drive down to Arugam. To really get to know the locals and their farm animals, jump a bus.

the perfect day   Four to six feet of southerly swell, light southwesterly winds.

best months   April–October.

boards   Your small-wave boards will get you out of trouble, but bring one more than you need, as good boards are rarer than flying elephants at this end of the coast.

essentials   Sunscreen and water in 44-gallon drums, and an ability to haggle with local taxi drivers.

accommodation   There's plenty, ranging from the upmarket Stardust Hotel all the way down to B&Bs charging just a handful of dollars a night.

other waves   Pottuvil Point is a few kilometres to the north, and Crocodile Rock 15 minutes to the south. If you have a good look around the area, you'll find plenty of good surf. In fact, if you're there in the off-season (November–March), the west coast around Hikkaduwa is the go.

bells beach
australia
sean doherty

Bells Beach is the spiritual home of surfing in Australia. No Australian wave has gathered more folklore and fantasy than the frosty, lurching walls of Bells. The beach itself may only be a couple of hundred metres long, but holds a special place in the hearts and minds of surfers around the world. The billowy legend of Bells may be writing cheques the wave itself has trouble cashing, however, as the place is often cold, inconsistent and crowded. When Patrick Swayze paddled out into the '50-year storm' at Bells Beach to commit aquatic hari-kiri at the end of the movie *Point Break*, the reality was that he was in more danger of dying from hypothermia or terminal cliché than from drowning (the surfing was actually filmed in Hawaii). But Bells is lacquered with so much history that surfing the place is like gracing the centre court at Wimbledon, or strolling 18 holes at St Andrews.

Bells Beach, named after the local farmer whose property the first surfers had to cross to get there in the 1950s, looks pretty much the same today as it did back then. Australia's first officially recognised surfing reserve, it's also part of the Point Addis Marine Park, and even on a good day the kangaroos and sheep outnumber the surfers 100 to one. And while a gaudy tourist Legoland scars the flashy point breaks of the Gold Coast, the golden-ochre cliffs of Bells face the vastness of the Southern

Ocean unmolested by development, just as they have for thousands of years.

Bells is the MCG of Australian surfing, and is the home of the world's longest-running professional surfing contest, the Rip Curl Pro. Since 1973, the Easter weekend at Bells has produced moments that have defined pro surfing in Australia. The schizophrenic brilliance of Michael Peterson winning the first three events from 1973 to 1975; the 1986 semi-final between Mark Occhilupo and Tom Curren, widely regarded as pro surfing's greatest-ever heat. However, 19 April 1981 trumps them all: 'Big Saturday' saw icy, 15-foot widow-makers storming in from the Antarctic to the stunned gathering of undergunned surfers. Seven world champions have won the Rip Curl Pro, and the respect it's held in was best summed up by 1998 winner, Hawaiian Shane Dorian, when he said, 'No kook ever wins Bells'.

The righthand point break at Bells has two distinct sections – Rincon and the Bells Bowl. Rincon is a racy, hotdog wave that zippers for 150 metres under the shadows of the Bells headland. It's best on a high tide, but will only handle swell up to four feet before it starts breaking on the wider section of the reef. The Bells Bowl is the *real* Bells: breaking in the middle of the bay between the headlands of Bells and Winkipop, it only starts showing itself at four feet but can handle anything up to 15 – and then some. The Bells Bowl offers up thick, sloping faces, and surfing the place when it's bigger seems more like snowboarding. Barrels are about as common as palm trees here, but open as the beach is to the full force of the Southern Ocean, the wave breaks with real punch. It's also a hard wave to master. The Bowl doesn't break top-to-bottom but does section off quickly, and even Kelly Slater readily admits that he's never really come to terms with it.

Despite the neighbouring towns of Torquay and Jan Juc being relatively small, the bad news is that pretty well everyone there surfs, and being only an hour away from Melbourne, Bells is always crowded. Ironically, though, there's actually a better wave than Bells that lives 300 metres across the bay to the east. Winkipop is a longer, faster righthand point, and on rare occasions when the swell is big the two waves will link up into one long, glorious life-changer. Get one of these and you'll be talked about in the front bar of the Torquay Hotel for years.

bells beach facts

location   Five minutes south of Torquay, off the Great Ocean Road, about 100 km southeast of Melbourne, Victoria.

getting there   Airports at Melbourne (90 minutes away) and Avalon (45 minutes away).

the perfect day   Eight feet of long-range southwest swell, combined with a light offshore northwest wind to clean it up. Let's make it a weekday, to keep the Melbournian crowds at home.

best months   March–June for the best swell/wind combo. Roaring 40s swells charge out of the Southern Ocean, but the winter storm winds haven't fully kicked in at this stage.

boards   Below six feet, add an inch or two to your standard shortboard. Over six feet, you'll need anything between a 6'4" and a 6'10". Boards with more volume are recommended, as the paddle out is long and gruelling.

essentials   A good wetsuit. For winter you'll need a 4/3 steamer and booties, and preferably a second dry one for the afternoon surf. In summer, a 2/3 steamer will get you by.

accommodation   The holiday towns of Torquay and Jan Juc have plenty of roofs — everything from houses to the local caravan park — to rest your surf-weary limbs under.

other waves   Along with nearby Winkipop, there's plenty of surf both up and down the coast. The Great Ocean Road to the southwest skirts some incredible coastline, and runs right past several quality reef, point and beach breaks. It's worth the drive even if there's no swell.

black rock
australia
sean doherty

Perched on the southern shores of Booderee National Park, this place is the definitive Australian surfing experience. As you hike along the track over the headland, the eucalypts slowly make way for banksias, the banksias make way for the ocean – and, if you've timed it right, a perfect, reefy lefthander. The vista you've got, an earthy montage of greens and blues and browns, is pretty well identical to the one the Wadi Wadi people, the place's traditional owners, would have surveyed 10000 years ago. While Black Rock remains a favourite day trip for Sydney surfers, what these guys are actually doing is driving back to another time. Compared to the grotty urban sink of Sydney, this place could be on another planet. If you are ever going to get a true appreciation of your place in the ancient and epic tale of Australia, it'll be here. And that's even before you've been barrelled.

To surfers, Black Rock is also known as Wreck Bay, Summercloud Bay, and good old Aussie Pipe. Wreck Bay is the name of the surrounding area; Summercloud, that of the smaller, adjoining bay; Black Rock's the break itself; and Aussie Pipe is the nickname. The Wreck Bay tag came from the handiwork of the aptly named Captain Nutter, who in 1835 managed to drive two boats – the *Hive* and the *Blackbird* – into the rocks off Bherwerre Beach within the space of a week. But the area's

European history is dwarfed by the importance of the area to the local Aborigines. Wreck Bay was part of the Jervis Bay National Park until it was renamed Booderee in 1997 and joint control was handed over to the Aboriginal community. Booderee means 'bay of plenty', which is exactly what it has been for the Wreck Bay Kooris for hundreds of generations.

Today, Black Rock is the home of Indigenous surfing in Australia, and a handful of Australia's best Koori surfers call the place home. Don't get embroiled in an argument about localism out here, because you'll never win, and there are no prizes for guessing which guys sit at the top of the pecking order out here. The exercise of surfing this place is, thankfully, a little simpler than the naming system. The wave itself is a peak, but it's the left that's the real deal. Best at four to six feet, it's a top-to-bottom backdoor barrel that hugs the corner of the reef, bending back in on itself as it rifles through to the inside, abruptly spilling its guts – and hopefully you – out into the deep water of the channel. Black Rock's odd combination of ideal conditions – a winter southerly swell with a summer northeast wind – means that it doesn't really have a 'season', and tends to be better in autumn and spring.

While the area is renowned for having the whitest sand in Australia, you'll be lucky to find a grain of it out here. They don't call it Black Rock for nothing, the place is the full reef platform. Although the barrel is generally so uniform that it's hard to screw it up, come off here and you'll lose skin. You get in and out of the water off the rocks inside the bay, which can also be a bit hairy as the ocean floor is blanketed with sea urchins. Stand on one of these and you'll know about it – you spend hours pulling out the spines with tweezers, thinking you've got them all, only for one to work its way out of your foot three months later. The place is also sharky as hell, but they're generally well fed and are content to just pop up three metres away just to frighten the hell out of you.

While Black Rock is the jewel of the New South Wales south coast, there are rich pickings in both directions. To see this incredible stretch of coastline properly, you need to slow yourself to the pace of the place, take a couple of weeks, and breathe it all in as you go.

black rock facts

location   South of Jervis Bay, 130 km south of Sydney on the south coast of New South Wales.

getting there   A four-hour drive from Sydney.

the perfect day   Four–six feet of southerly swell, light northeast winds, midweek crowds.

best months   October–May, as the winter southerly winds blow straight through the place.

boards   A shortboard with a bit of volume, and nothing too skatey, as the wave has punch and pretty well all you'll be doing is pulling in.

essentials   A board, a wetsuit, and no other valuables to leave in your car. Owing to the remoteness of the car park, the place has a bad reputation for car rip-offs.

accommodation   There are plenty of amazing camping grounds in the area, which are the best way to soak up the place. For most of the year, wallabies outnumber campers.

other waves   Take your pick. Black Rock is a great wave, but the area is littered with quality reef breaks and points. Green Island, Ulladulla Bommie and Bawley Point are all only an hour away.

bundoran peak
ireland
craig jarvis

Bundoran is the heart of surfing in Ireland, and Bundoran Peak is the main wave in town. It has been featured in so many surf magazines and videos that any surfer worth his or her salt knows exactly what the area is like, what the waves are like, and where the Bridge Bar is. The thing is, though, those mags get it wrong and the videos also tell a few lies. These waves, including the Bundoran left, are extremely rare, and the number of variables you have to deal with to get them is exhausting. It is a wild stretch of coastline, exposed to big storms, and the area is also extremely tidal. We're not going to list all the negatives; suffice it to say that Bundoran is not consistent at all. Still, when it gets good it gets very good.

The area has had a few problems over the last few years, what with the pushing of a marina development right where the wave is. Despite the fact that this proposal has been squashed twice in a campaign spearheaded by local surfer and surf-shop owner Richie Fitsgerald, it still exists in some murky office somewhere and is bound to resurface. The marina would have taken out the best wave and the very reason why so many surfers come to Bundoran. In 2001, a gathering of legendary surfers and ex-world-champions surfed off here in the ISA World Masters competition, with Gary Elkerton winning the Masters and Mark Richards the Grandmasters divisions.

The wave in Bundoran is the Peak, a long barrelling left and a short, more intense right that barrels as well. It works best on a low tide (and, as stated, this area is extremely tidal), when the swell is small. As the swell gets bigger, the wave starts to go right through the tides; but if it gets massive, the left becomes quite difficult and all attention turns to the right. The right breaks into a deep channel, so it won't close out when it gets big and you can still paddle out across the bay. While sitting out at backline you'll see a few other waves in the distance – a left that breaks near the harbour and another left that breaks just down the road. They both can get quite epic in certain conditions and can actually rival the Peak for full-on barrels.

Despite the fact that there are only two real surf shops in town, and it is normally always raining, when the waves at the Peak are good a lot of surfers emerge from the woodwork or from nearby towns. It can get really crowded, so if you're a blow-in you'll find yourself quite low in the pecking order. It shouldn't take too long to get to know the local crew, though, as most of them head straight for the pub as soon as a session is over, and they're all pretty genuine, hearty people. Share a couple of pints of Guinness with them and you'll be getting some waves the next swell.

The area around Bundoran is also home to some big outside bombies and a couple of tow crew have been sniffing around, getting some good ones, getting skunked a few times. The Emerald Isle, despite the coldness and other vagaries, is something of a hidden gem and hasn't revealed all yet.

bundoran peak facts

location　In County Donegal on the northwest coast of Ireland.

getting there　Fly to Dublin or catch a ferry from Wales or the UK.

the perfect day　Light southeast winds, west swell of four–six feet, pushing tide. Late in the year, when the water is still warm(ish).

best months　August–October, sometimes as late as November. The waves carry on through the winter, but it gets too cold for human tolerance.

boards　Generally a few small boards and maybe a semi-gun. If you're going to stay the winter, a gun or two is recommended because breakages are likely.

essentials　Top-of-the-range wetsuit with boots, glove and hood. Your wetsuit is by far the most important surfing gear in Ireland, so it's pointless skimping.

accommodation　Lots of places to stay. For a start, you could contact Tyrconnell Holiday Homes.

other waves　Plenty of waves in the immediate vicinity, such as Tullen and Black Spot. And a few others that you have to search for.

burleigh heads
australia
sean doherty

The only surfers happier than the Coolangatta locals about the birth of the Superbank in 2001 were the Burleigh boys, 15 minutes up the coast. The Superbank has become a saltwater circus, and allowed the hypnotic blue tubes of Burleigh Heads to slink back into the shadows. Considering Burleigh's been in the surfing limelight for 30 years, this sudden relative anonymity suits the Burleigh locals just fine, thanks very much. If this were anywhere else in the world, Burleigh would be a surfing shrine, but on a stretch of surf coast so embarrassingly rich, it is just another ho-hum perfect righthand point break.

While the Superbank has five years of history to dwell upon, Burleigh's roots are a little more ancient. The headland was formed 22 million years ago when the volcano Mount Warning produced the lava flow that eventually formed the giant basalt bluff that now stands sentinel over the break. Unfortunately the natural beauty of Burleigh didn't last long once white fellas got hold of it. You can take off on a wave behind the Cove without seeing a sign of man's handiwork, only to kick out 30 seconds later in front of the highest concentration of tourist concrete anywhere in the southern hemisphere.

Like all the Gold Coast point breaks, Burleigh is heavily reliant on sand flow. No matter how exquisitely sculpted the point itself might be for the purposes of creating righthand barrels, if the sand's askew you might as well be going left. Fortunately, the banks at Burleigh are fed from the creek mouth at Tallebudgera on the south side of the headland, and the sand is generally fine-grained and packed like mortar.

The wave begins out the front of the headland at the Cove section, which is characterised by fast-moving currents and a shallow sand-shelf. Once through the Cove, the wave corners the point, following the contour of the black boulders, before racing off again down the beach. The famed Burleigh barrel is a very different beast to its mate down the coast at Kirra, and has a more chummy quality to it. As far as size goes, Burleigh starts breaking at two feet and will hold eight and then some, particularly if the swell is coming more out of the south.

As with Lennox Head, the most dangerous part of surfing Burleigh is getting off the rocks lining the Cove. They are coated in a thin film of algae, and trying to hop from one to another induces a sensation not unlike wearing rollerskates while mountain-climbing. If you slip off one, you'll end up wedged down between them until the next wave steams through and pinballs you, damaging body, board and ego.

Burleigh is home to some of the most parochial and hardcore surfers you'll ever come across, many of whom are inked up proudly with the town's 4220 postcode. Despite the Superbank stealing the hype, the crowd here on a good day will have you believing that the local unemployment rate is nudging triple figures. Although Burleigh has produced several world-class surfers and was the birthplace of man-on-man surfing (during the Stubbies event in 1977), on any given day there'll be a small army of guys you've never heard of who will surf rings around the blow-ins. Peter Harris did just this when the world's best surfers congregated here in 1980. Harris, the local postman, surfed all the way to the title and then went back to delivering the mail.

But while man can cover the headland in buildings and create his own perfect sandbank, the pandanus palms, black volcanic marbles, ice-blue water and rifling tubes of Burleigh will be at least one constant in the ever-changing Gold Coast landscape.

burleigh heads facts

location   Gold Coast, Queensland.

getting there   Fly to Coolangatta airport, from where it's a 15-minute drive north.

the perfect day   Six feet of southeast swell, light southwest winds.

best months   February through to August, as Burleigh will break well in cyclonic northerly swells as well as traditional winter southerly swells.

boards   A solid shortboard will do the trick. You'll be doing a heap of tube riding, so you don't want too big a board.

essentials Patience to deal with the crowd.

accommodation   Just turn around and look. If you can't find accommodation in this tourist megalopolis you'll also need directions to find your big toe.

other waves   Plenty of 'em . . . and they're all righthand points. Heading south you'll run into (in order) Currumbin, Kirra and the Superbank. Or you can drive for a whole exhausting hour down to Lennox Head. If you want to go left, you'll have to travel a bit further.

cave rock
south africa
craig jarvis

Cave Rock is just a few kilometres from Durban, on South Africa's southeast coast. Seafront, subtropical Durban is also known to many as 'Surf City'.

The town waves of Durban get tempered somewhat near the northern arm of the harbour wall, all but blocking swells from the south and southwest. The Bluff, the stretch of coast that is home to Cave Rock, receives the full brunt of these swells and revels in them. The waves are more powerful than the Durban waves, and break over a rock-and-sand combo. It is the refuge for competitive surfers who have been knocked out of a contest in town, and it is also very photogenic.

Despite being just a short drive from Durban, the Bluff has a different feel and personality altogether, and the people who live there are somewhat different to their town neighbours as well. The friendly rivalry that exists between the 'rough and tough and from the Bluff' boys and the 'town clowns' has been going on forever and is not about to be settled any time soon, but it is just that – a friendly, competitive rivalry. People who live on the Bluff tend to stay there, preferring the bigger, more powerful surf on their doorsteps and rarely venturing into town unless the swell on their side is maxing out. Rudy Palmboom is one such local, who at the age of 48 has never really left the Bluff and has surfed it on pretty well every good day. Rudy, who was a familiar of Shaun Tomson's, decided to stay put on the Bluff when Shaun went off to Hawaii for the first time. Rudy has a son, Rudy Junior, and a daughter, Heidi, who both rip under the watchful eye of their mum Tersia.

Cave Rock is the jewel in the crown on this little stretch of coast, named after a huge, flat rock that sits right in front of the wave. Although there are a couple of waves right there, it is the reef section which squares out and throws some thick, gnarly barrels – that garners the most attention. It is possible to get into the wave early on a big day and set yourself up for the barrel section, but it takes a fair amount of fortitude to pull in when it hits the shelf.

Cave Rock has been home to a couple of specialty surfing events, most notably the Rip Curl Tubemasters. An invitation-only event, Cave Rock usually delivers some sick barrels over the waiting period. Lately it has been pretty low-key, with no events and a fairly average season or two. Still, due to the location of the Bluff, many epic sessions go unnoticed by surfers and photographers, and local riders just glut on the barrels. The waves in the immediate vicinity also lend themselves to the name 'Cave Rock', such as the section of wave that breaks behind the tidal pool and also throws some thick barrels. On the other side there is a beach-break section that, on the right day, delivers longer and cleaner barrels than the reef itself.

Cave Rock is a pretty serious wave. There have been many broken boards and limbs, and one surfing-related death. There are also some sharks around, so be aware of your dimensions.

Cave Rock is the jewel in the crown on this little stretch of coast, named after a huge, flat rock that sits right in front of the wave.

cave rock facts

location On the Bluff, just south of Durban on the KwaZulu–Natal coast. If you're sitting in the water in Durban, facing out to sea, the 'mountain' to your right, directly behind the harbour entrance, is the Bluff.

getting there From Durban airport (18 km south of town) it's just a short drive to the Bluff.

the perfect day Six-foot southerly swell from far away, light northwest land breeze, low tide pushing. Boardshorts. Girls on the beach. It all happens quite often, actually.

best months March–June. Land breeze is regular and there is plenty of swell.

boards A few small boards and a semi-gun. Cave Rock is a solid wave and gets big, but there are lots of days on the Bluff when the waves are fun and rippable beach breaks.

essentials Boardshorts, or possibly a shortie in winter. Suncream, and lots of it.

accommodation Ansteys Beach Backpackers, right on the beach at Ansteys, the main beach break in the area. Owned by the Palmboom family, it offers surfing lessons too.

other waves Plenty, for all tastes. Local spots include Ansteys Beach, Brighton Beach and Pigg's Hut. This little stretch of coast is wave-rich, almost like Hawaii's North Shore.

chicama
peru
matt griggs

Four kilometres! (Yes, you heard right.) It's probably fitting that Chicama is the longest left wave in the world, because from no matter where you've come, there's nothing short about getting there. You've either come all the way across the world's biggest ocean (the Pacific), down or up the driest desert coast in the world, along the world's longest road (the Pan-American Highway), or over the top of the world's second-greatest mountain range (the Andes).

Peru is a land of extremes and, for surfers, Chicama is its big daddy – a series of long points that wrap and link below the sandy cliffs of the desert. The water is cold, thanks to the Antarctic current hitching a ride up the west coast of South America. The wind is consistently offshore (offshore is the only wind that has ever blown here), and the windmills upon her cliffs vouch for its strength, powering the local town's electricity with as much ease as they hold up the barrel.

Because they can't afford surfboards (as in most third-world countries), the two or three local surfers ride old boards that are left as presents by tourists. Generally these have been broken or are in need of repair, but the locals are stoked just to be able to surf – and they share their waves and their experiences with equal enthusiasm. One day I sat with Jesus, one of the local surfers; he's a natural footer, but quickly learned how to surf goofy as well. The swell was around two–three feet but really lined up – we counted seventeen waves from start to finish. If there were a ruler big enough, you could have drawn a perfectly straight line from the pier to the take-off spot, three kilometres away.

The Chicama wave makes for interesting mind-surfing, but the real thing can be a little more tiresome. There is so much room and space on this wave that you have the opportunity to try anything, several hundred times in one session. You literally take off, do about ten turns, relax, stand there for a while, catch your breath – and do it again . . . and again . . . and again. If all the points link up, it's a ride of over five kilometres, but this doesn't happen – and don't believe anyone who says otherwise. There are three points, all world-class, that angle back towards the town. The swell is your nemesis, losing its top as it wraps around the bay (a swell of six–eight feet will be four feet here), but positions itself perfectly again afterwards for the trip down to the pier. Even at three feet, waves roll mechanically, rhythmically, methodically and magically down the point, hypnotising surfers to salivation. You could probably make the whole five-kilometre journey in about five waves, tops!

Only 700 years ago the Incas roamed this area – and their mystery and magic is enshrined in the desert sand. There has never been a big professional event here; there haven't been many professional surfers. It's not that sort of place. It's just a place for people willing to climb over, across and through some of the world's greatest natural wonders, to find one of surfing's holy grails.

chicama facts

location   600 km north of Lima, Peru's capital city.

getting there   Fly to Lima, after which you'll need to hire a car or chance a bus for the six-hour drive on a very crazy road.

the perfect day   Big south swells. It will hold almost anything, but six–eight feet is perfect. The wind is always offshore, so you just need a swell big enough to get around the corner of the bay.

best months   Late March–September

boards   You only really need a shortboard and maybe a groveller for Chicama, but a trip to Peru will offer chances to ride everything up to 20-foot waves. It depends the sort of waves you are inclined to ride.

essentials   A good wetsuit – the water here is cold.

accommodation   There are a few B&B-type places on the beach, which are very rarely booked up. They all offer views over the point at a very affordable price.

other waves   Pacasmayo (a 20-minute drive away) is the other point. It picks up more swell and is almost as long as Chicama. Between the two, you'll be a very happy surfer.

cloud nine
the philippines
matt griggs

'It's definitely one of the most perfect and mechanical waves I have ever surfed,' says Mark Mathews, a former winner of the professional event that happens here once a year. It may be mechanical and predictable – and found in a place often referred to as the 'Ficklepines' – but when Cloud Nine does its thing you'll soon forget any negative connotations and give in to its peerless perfection. Located on one of 7017 islands that make up the Philippines, Cloud Nine is open to whatever the western Pacific can dish up. It's a turbulent area, weather-wise, and it is these localised storms that produce most of the swell from August to October. If you're really lucky, you'll have a typhoon swell brewing in the South China Sea – there are usually around 10–20 of these a year, ranging from mini typhoons to super versions with winds of up to 300 km/h that have enough power to make Mack trucks roll like tumbleweeds.

The first publicised trip to Cloud Nine was back in 1992, by photographer John Callahan and Californian surfers Taylor Knox and Evan Slater. But they weren't the first here: it takes a certain type of eccentricity to explore this place, and that was evident in its discoverer, Mike Boyum (who also discovered Grajagan). On the run from Hawaiian authorities (and most probably a host of underworld forces) on drug charges and going by the name 'Max Walker', he arrived at nearby Tuason Point in January 1988. Living alone in a beachfront bungalow, Boyum embarked on a 47-day cleansing fast, but a priest who had arranged to meet him on the 47th day walked in to discover that Boyum had died three days earlier, on his birthday.

There are other waves around if you need to break the monotony, but none is anywhere near the class of Cloud Nine. Because most of the islands are unexplored by surfers, there is plenty of opportunity, but you would need a lot of time to test the theory. There is quite a local surfing contingent developing at Cloud Nine now, thanks to travelling surfers leaving behind boards (generally broken ones) that they use. They're a fun-loving bunch and are generally just as happy to watch you catch a wave as to hassle you. Because they are largely uninfluenced by surfers for most of the year, don't see surf videos and ride battered boards, they have developed a tricky style that reflects their unique island character. You'll see them switch-footing, and pulling in, in quite new ways.

The wind can shuffle around here because you get a lot of local storm activity, but if you don't like what the wind is doing, stick around for ten minutes and it will probably swing back to offshore. Even at two to three feet, Cloud Nine is fun – it still barrels, but in terms of power per square inch, you get a lot of bang for your buck. When it's four–six feet, it is absolutely perfect – the ultimate barrel/cutback combo. You take off behind the peak, backdoor through the whole section – which breaks in the same spot every time – and come flying out into a little horseshoe section with so much speed that all you can do is bury the rail into the biggest cutback you can muster. The take-off gets a little trickier the bigger the wave; if it hits eight feet, it starts washing through a little and turns into more of a left. But it rarely gets this big – and even when it does, you'll still be out there looking for diamonds in the rough.

cloud nine facts

location   On the island of Siargao in the Philippines, 800 km south of Manila.

getting there   It's simplest to fly to Manila and/or Cebu, and from there direct to Siargao or via Surigao (cheaper but longer, as boats more frequent than planes). It's then a bus or jeepney ride to Cloud Nine.

the perfect day   Mid to low tide, six to eight feet.

best months   Late March–September

boards   Shortboard, or 2 inches longer. The wave is fast and critical, so too much board won't fit in the pocket. You can ride a bigger board if that's the way you like to ride the barrel, but it isn't really needed.

essentials   Protection! You are on the Equator, so you'll need sunscreen, rashies and plenty of mosquito repellent.

accommodation   There is plenty of bungalow-style accommodation here, but the best is Segana Resort, situated right in front of the break.

other waves   If you have to — the waves around Cloud aren't as good as those of the outer islands. Better to get on a boat and really explore the Philippines. You can email scottcountryman@yahoo.com to climb on board his epic vessel.

cloudbreak
fiji
sean doherty

It's ironic that the surfing world's most exclusive and lucrative surf camps began life as one of its great grass-roots discoveries. When American surfer Dave Clarke stumbled across Fiji's Tavarua Island in the early 1980s he knew he was onto a good thing. Camping out on the uninhabited island and surfing the racy lefts of (what would much later become known as) Restaurants, it wasn't long before he looked out to sea and noticed a spinning left breaking on an outer reef a few kilometres away. Twenty-five years later Tavarua is inhabited by an exclusive resort, and the wave Clark saw on the horizon – Cloudbreak – has become the world's most controversial wave.

To surf Cloudbreak today you must be a guest on Tavarua. The debate about the private control of surf breaks began here, the first wave to have access to it exclusively controlled. The concept of 'owning' part of the ocean doesn't sit too well with many surfing purists, who argue that sunshine and fresh air will be the next commodities to be sold off in package deals. However, the island and the surrounding reefs and fishing grounds have been owned and controlled by the local Fijian people for thousands of years, and considering the village is a partner in the resort venture, the counter-argument is that the exclusivity arrangement is just the Fijian way of doing things. Either way, if you're going to include this one on your list you're not going to get out of it cheaply, and you may need a long-lost aunt to pass away and leave you the family estate in the south of France to finance your trip.

Controversy aside, Cloudbreak is quite a piece of work. Perched on Viti Levu's barrier reef, Cloudbreak was named for its spectral appearance as the distant plumes of spray merge with the horizon. If the sight of eight-foot waves on the horizon doesn't loosen up last night's fish dinner, check your pulse – you may be dead. The wave itself breaks like a point break, a very long, heavy, reefy point that can run up to 300 metres. Peaking on a section of reef known as the Ledge, the wave builds and coils, allowing a couple of big turns before turning itself inside-out across the main barrel section. If you emerge in one piece, the wave will then wall up again and start to race away from you as it works its way into the end section, Shishkebabs. At this point you may notice the crystal-blue water that's been whizzing past you since you took off suddenly turn a mission-brown colour, as the wave begins to run out of water. Due to the constant wave action, the reef here is not nearly as sharp as nearby Restaurants, but it's no pillow factory either, and has the potential to make a real mess of your modelling contract if you roll around on it.

The thing with Cloudbreak is that everything is big – the reef, the currents, the swell. It's a surfing Land of the Giants, so it's no surprise that Cloudbreak handles some real size and is home to some of the southern hemisphere's biggest rideable surf. Southwest groundswells from below Australia work their way up and train themselves on the corner of the reef at Cloudbreak, and the scope of the reef means it can handle 20-foot surf. Hawaiian hellman Shane Dorian actually works part of the year as a surf guide on Tavarua (coincidentally, right in peak-swell season), and during his hiatus from the pro tour Kelly Slater toyed with the idea of living on the island. If, however, you'd rather chew your own arms down to bloody stumps than paddle out at 12-foot Cloudbreak, then you're in luck, because at the same time Restaurants, five minutes away, will be firing at five feet. And if that prospect is still turning you palm-tree green, back on Tavarua the bar will surely be offshore.

cloudbreak facts

location   Tavarua Island, in the Mamanuea island group, three km from the main Fijian island of Viti Levu.

getting there   Fly to Nadi, where you'll be shuttled out by bus and then longboat to Tavarua.

the perfect day   Eight to 10 feet of clean southwest swell, light southeast trade winds.

best months   The local dry season, April–September.

boards   Think of it as a trip to Indo and pack boards accordingly. Cloudbreak can handle pretty well any swell thrown at it, so along with your standard shortboards you'll need a couple of bigger boards, between 6'6" and 6'10".

essentials   As you'll be staying on Tavarua, pretty well everything is there for you.

accommodation   You'll be doing it in style if you're a Tavarua guest. However, every Saturday – 'Changeover Day' – Tavarua relaxes the rules and allows a boatload of surfers from nearby islands the chance to come and surf Cloudbreak.

other waves   The Tavarua-controlled waves of Restaurants and Tavvy Rights, and nearby Wilkes Pass and Desperations for all comers.

COXOS
portugal
ben mondy

Along with Hossegor's beach breaks and Mundaka's river-mouth tubes, the thundering reef rights of Coxos are firmly established as one of Europe's surfing jewels. Coxos lies at the heart of all things surfing in Portugal, with the country's best wave, not surprisingly, hosting the country's hottest surfers. Current professionals José Gregório, Paulo do Bairro, Ruben Gonsalves, Aecio Flavio and last, but not least, Tiago Pires, all name Coxos as their favourite break. Tiago is pretty much the Kelly Slater of Portuguese surfing, a man that has only failed to make the World Championship Tour about three times, and then by the faintest of whiskers.

Tiago's surfing, like all the other rippers from round here, has been harnessed and shaped by the local waves – which happen to be thick and powerful, and none come thicker or more powerful than at Coxos. In addition, surfing is an intrinsic part of the community fabric around this part of the world, like it is in Sydney or Santa Cruz or Margaret River. But that shouldn't come as a surprise. The Portuguese are famous seafarers, with the likes of Vasco de Gama and Ferdinand Magellan departing Lisbon in the 15th century to roam the then-uncharted waters as far afield as Indonesia and Australia. With one whole coast bordered by the Atlantic, and with the ocean providing the main source of income and food, it's no wonder that the Portuguese took to surfing.

That said, it takes something special to take to Coxos. The wave itself is a challenging beast that doesn't really start to show form until the swell hits six feet; it can hold up to 10 feet, and then some. One of the more famous recorded sequences of the wave featured an 18-year-old Joel Parkinson somehow holding his edge through a throttling Coxos tube that his pro surfing mates, watching slack-jawed from the car park overlooking the break, labelled an easy 12 'Hawaiian feet'.

But the wave itself is probably best at around eight feet, when powerful northwest swells formed from deep lows in the North Atlantic are scrubbed clean and raw by a southeasterly offshore and twisted into shape by the urchin-infested, ultra-sharp volcanic reef below. A heart-in-mouth drop is followed by a big barrel section, which if negotiated successfully opens up into a whackable wall and, down the line, a few more barrel opportunities. Waves can repeat this cycle for as long as 400 metres, giving you the choice of a jelly-arm paddle back out, or a bolt back to the point, where a treacherous jump-off (don't be fooled by how easy the locals make it look) awaits.

With a wave of this quality, it's no surprise that there's a strong local scene. The pros mentioned above were well schooled by the preceding generation, and on a good day a hardcore bunch of blokes who have been surfing here for over two decades enjoy enormous respect. Though, if the vans of travelling surfers from around the world show the same type of regard, they are usually rewarded with quality waves. And if you time it right, typically in the colder winter months and during the week, crowds aren't the problem. You are much better off worrying yourself with the 'set *cabrão*' – Coxos' notorious clean-up sets that you can pretty much count on to rag-doll you for about 100 metres at least once a session, in a high-speed underwater torture test. Still, that's just part of the deal – it's a heavy wave with heavy consequences. The rewards, though – well, the rewards are what make Coxos one of the world's most sought-after surf spots.

coxos

location   Just north of the town of Ericeira, about 50 km north of Portugal's capital, Lisbon.

getting there   Fly into Lisbon airport, which is only a 45-minute drive away.

The perfect day   A midweek November morning sees sunny skies, offshore winds, 17°C water and an eight-foot swell. Following your second three-hour session, you'll head for cheap, amazing seafood washed down with cheap cold beers as the sun goes down into the sea.

best months   October–March. While a little chilly, the consistent swell and small crowds will keep you content.

boards   The full quiver, from shortboard to big guns. This wave has serious range.

essentials   A taste for seafood. And some good locks on your car – the car park is known as thieving hotspot.

accommodation   There's a camping ground nearby, plus two surf camps and a heap of cheap *pensions* (apartments) and hotels in town.

other waves   Ericeira is chock-full of quality reefs, the most famous being Pedro Banço, the Reef, and the Bells doppelgänger Ribeira D'ihas.

desert point
lombok
ben mondy

The debate over which is the world's best wave is almost as old as surfing itself. You can just imagine the ancient Hawaiian chiefs arguing the merits of their respective breaks over a post-surf feast of wild boar, pineapple and naked virgins. Yet whenever the discussion rears up again – be it between mates or in magazines – it's a pretty safe bet that Desert Point, the fabled left on the Indonesian island of Lombok, will be one of the first waves to be tossed into the mix.

You see, this wave has almost mystical status for those who have surfed it. Even in Indonesia, the home of the perfect left, it stands out as being simply the most perfect tube any surfer could imagine. This is a wave that can make a daydreaming schoolboy's pencil-case drawing of a consummate wave look like a fat, flawed, close-out. On a good day, surfers have been known to be barrelled for more than 20 seconds, and Desert aficionados brag of six proper five-second tubes on the one wave. It's no small wonder that *Tracks* voted it number one in their '100 Best Waves of the World' back in 2000.

If this all sounds too good to be true, well, that's because it kind of is. Desert's eminence has been enhanced – like a signed Jimi Hendrix guitar, or a Gold Coast virgin – by its rarity. This is by no means a consistent wave, and a number of often-elusive factors have to all come together at the same time for it to turn on. A massive, just-right southwest swell has to coincide with a band of tide that happens only a few days each month. Yet even then, with all of Desert's planets aligned in some type of cosmic order, strange things can happen. Massive lulls will destroy the line-up, or one of the strongest sweeps on Earth will pick you up, whisking you out at 40 knots past the take-off zone and into one of the world's deepest and most dangerous stretches of water, Lombok Strait. But like an abusive lover, all is forgotten as soon as, magically, Desert switches on. An easy take-off launches you into a perfectly pitching, ever-growing wave. The razor-sharp coral gets closer and closer to your fins as you progress, leading to a point where either you are locked in for one of the most orgasmic tubes of your life or you cop a strafing across a live, bacteria-filled cheese grater.

In the early days, such was the magnetic attraction of the wave, surfers would camp there for months at a time, enduring the harsh, dry landscape (it isn't called Desert Point for nothing), the long flat spells, the malaria-filled mosquitoes and the primitive isolation all for the sweet days of perfection. And many a Desert diehard who, after many a long bleak season, became quite proprietorial about 'their' wave. But the increasing number of charter boats travelling from Bali to Sumbawa changed that, and by the late 90s a Desert's swell would see many vessels anchored up. There was a little local unrest, culminating in some camping surfers being attacked with knives, which eventually made staying on the beach less of an option.

These days, it has settled down. Coupled with the accuracy of internet forecasting this means, however, that when Desert's is on a lot of people are onto it. In the 2006 winter season, for example, crowds of 50 people were not uncommon on good days. So is it crowded? Yes. Is it fickle? Yes. Is it the best wave in the world? Go and find out for yourself.

desert point facts

location　Southwest coast of the island of Lombok, which is just a few km east of Bali.

getting there　Fly into Denpasar, then either car and ferry it to Lombok, or take a domestic flight to Mataram. A 4WD is highly recommended for the drive.

the perfect day　It's six feet and offshore, and without a hint of a rip or sweep. Lombok Strait has waylaid all the charter boats, and there is just a handful of you surfing the best tubes in Indo.

best months　May–September. As in the rest of Indonesia, the southeast trade winds are now blowing and offshore.

boards　No turns, just tubes here, folks, so there is no need for the rhino chaser. Normal shortboards, just maybe a little narrower and pinnier.

essentials　Suncream, tee-shirt, large gonads, first-aid kit, tube sense.

accommodation　There is some good, cheap, losmen-style accommodation in the neighbouring town of Bangko Bangko, but a new five-star holiday resort has been approved in the area.

other waves　There are other waves on Lombok, but they are a long, long drive away and nowhere near the quality. You are here for only one break – Desert's.

gnaraloo
australia
ben mondy

Is there a harsher, deadlier, heavier and more perfect wave in Australia than Gnaraloo? Pronounced 'nar-loo' (I mean, it even sounds gnarly) this heaving slab of a lefthander is located about three hours drive from the outback town of Carnarvon in Western Australia.

If your body, vehicle and supplies survive the potholed road and kamikaze kangaroos, you'll then be faced with one of the sternest tests that surfing has to offer, and that's before you even hit the water. With the break so far removed from any form of civilisation, most trips here necessitate a fairly lengthy stay, which involves setting up a camp in the extremely harsh, fly-ridden desert. Preparation is paramount, and monitoring your water, food, medical and, most importantly, beer supplies is essential.

While the question of who was first to surf Gnaraloo is still debated, hard-core surfers have been travelling here since the early 70s. Initially, one of surfing's best-kept secrets was kept secret owing to its sheer isolation. However, surfers being surfers, the outstanding quality of the wave was soon being whispered in surfing-town pubs and car parks. The crowds increased slowly, mainly driven by the increasing surfing population in and around Perth and Margaret River. For them, it was a tantalising yin/yang proposition – the same winter storms that batter those southern spots, lashing the coast with huge swells, onshore winds and ferocious rain, provide Gnaraloo, 1200 kilometres away, with trade-wind-like offshores and consistent, groomed swells. Throughout the 80s and 90s, surfers would set up base in the desert for three months at a time. A community would evolve there, connected by getting tubed, catching fish, avoiding getting eaten by sharks, mosquitoes and scorpions, and generally living a primitive, utopian surfing dream.

But as with most modern phenomena, especially ones involving mind-bendingly powerful tubes, the situation couldn't last. For many, the tipping point was Billabong's groundbreaking Challenges, the first of which took place in Gnaraloo in 1995 and featured Kelly Slater, Rob Machado, Sunny Garcia and Occy, among others. The eight-foot grinders, the blue-green light and the new competition format were all captured masterfully on video by Jack McCoy, and the film's success meant that all of a sudden a whole lot more people knew just how good a surfing spot this place was. The crowds have grown since then, along with the facilities; and the camping ground now sells limited supplies and imposes an additional charge for your dog (this being, for many diehards, the final death knell).

But some things don't change, and luckily for us these just happen to be the harsh desert environment and the heavy, ledging tubes, both still offering a true test of character and keeping crowds manageable. The wave actually features two distinct breaks. There is an outside ledge, called Centresides, which provides a slightly easier, shorter and more perfect barrel. But for the fanatics – guys like Paul Donda, Mike Macauliffe, Dave Macaulay and Paul 'Antman' Patterson – surfing Gnaraloo is all about Tombstones, or 'Tombies'. This is in fact a wave that incorporates three unique ledges along its 300-metre, roller-coaster stretch of fear and exhilaration. An intimidating, balls-in-throat drop is followed by a series of negotiations with Huey and the hard coral below, which, if successful, can land you in the channel with three world-class barrels under your belt and a smile like a split watermelon.

Of course, if you screw it up, a whole world of pain awaits. Surfers as good as Jim Banks, Martin Potter and Antman Paterson all have horrific tales of broken bones, ligaments and cartilage out here, a testament to the raw power and unpredictability of the place.

gnaraloo facts

location   Far northwest coast of Western Australia.

getting there   Fly into Perth and drive from there (about 10 hours) or fly on to Carnarvon and hire a car. For the drive, a 4WD is recommended.

the perfect day   An eight-foot swell is rattling over the reef, made slightly less daunting by a large high tide. A small crowd, and it's the last day of your two months in the desert.

best months   June–September, when there are sunny skies, consistent swells and offshore winds. Summer here is hell – 45°C, no swell, and howling onshores.

boards   It's all about the barrel here, so you'll need a quiver of shortboards and semi-guns. Make them extra-thick, though, as this place devours fibreglass.

essentials   4WD, tent, plenty of water, and *ER*-style first-aid kit.

accommodation   Provide your own, with campsites around $20 a night.

other waves   There's the notorious Bommie across the channel; Midges, a made-for-tow-in left up the reef; Monuments, a world-class super-shallow right; and Fencelines and Turtles for light relief. Oh, and the Bluff, another of the world's best lefts, is half an hour away.

grajagan
java
dave sparkes

The impossibly long, lefthand reef of Grajagan is truly one of the surfing world's first exotics. At a time when Bali was still like another planet, Grajagan (or 'G-Land', as it's commonly known) was another universe. It was the early 70s, and the warm, perfect surf of Bali, featuring the epic lefts of Uluwatu, as well as great food, cheap living, and hyper-friendly people, were the realisation of your archetypal surfer's dream. Very few people would have bothered to try to improve on this ideal scenario, but a chance plane ride tickled at least one adventurous surfer's itch.

In 1972, American Bob Laverty was flying south to Bali and happened to glance down as the plane arced over southwestern Java. What he saw created a new reference point for surfers, as the majestic wrap of the two-kilometre-long Grajagan reef presented itself in full flight, with unbroken lines of flawless lefts running far down into the bay. When he got to Bali, Laverty went on a recruiting drive; he was determined to go to Java, to find and sample that awesome set-up. He had few takers, however, understandable given the paradise that was Bali in 1972. But he found a willing soul in Bill Boyum, and within days they biked, boated, hiked and crawled their way to the break, finally collapsing on the beach as darkness descended. The shore skirts a dense, pristine jungle, rumoured to contain everything from tigers (doubtful) to leopards and monkeys (certainly), and the cacophony of wildlife noises was their unsettling but exotic sleep soundtrack. The next morning they awoke to spitting eight-foot barrels, and the legend was born.

For a couple of years, Grajagan remained a whispered rumour, a metaphorical big sister to Uluwatu, and many believed it was just a myth. Around 1974, however, Bill Boyum's brother Mike set up what was probably the world's first surf camp, a Spartan affair which allowed surfers to subsist – just – and surf what was becoming known as the world's best left. Eventually Balinese surfer Bobby Radiasa took over the camp, and he is still running it. There is also another camp these days, but it doesn't match the sophistication of Bobby's, with its satellite TV, cinema, and decadent ration of eight beers a day. Of course, the monkeys are still there and still as mischievous as ever.

As with most legendary breaks, the name Grajagan is intertwined with those of legendary surfers. Gerry Lopez parlayed his Mr Pipeline title to become probably the favourite son of G-Land, fitting his silky-smooth, casual approach into the wave like a hand into a glove, and to this day he continues to return there. Others to stamp their names on the freight-train barrels are Peter McCabe, Luke Egan and Tom Carroll, and there is a supporting cast of underground chargers like Sloth, Camel and many others.

The waves rear up and assault the reef with Hawaii-like power, caressed by southeast trade winds.

Located on the southern tip of the Blambungan Peninsula, Grajagan receives the brunt of southern winter swells travelling up through the Indian Ocean. Steaming in from three-kilometre-deep water just offshore, the waves rear up and assault the reef with Hawaii-like power, caressed by southeast trade winds. The outermost section, Kongs, throws up open-faced ski

slopes, perfect for long lines and big turns. A couple of hundred metres down the line the Money Trees section kicks in, hosting beautiful almond-shaped barrels for 200 metres. It's the bread-and-butter section, the most consistent of the G-Land family and usually surfable. As Money Trees loses its angle, Launching Pads rears up into big wedges, which as its name suggests are the best entry point into the real reason tube junkies go to G-Land: Speedies. This is serious business, as 300 metres of draining, shallow tubes suck and spiral down the razor-sharp coral reef. Tube rides of 15–20 seconds are not out of the question here; but, of course, any errors have serious consequences, and the number of sutures required over the years due to this section can be counted in the thousands. Beware.

While retaining its aura of mystery and isolation, and its big jungle cats, these days G-Land can get crowded. The advent of internet swell-predicting means surfers can hang out in more comfortable Bali, and bolt over to G-Land in the blink of an eye when a swell looms. But with a line-up stretching to around a kilometre, there is still room to move on this vast and incomparable natural racetrack.

grajagan facts

location In the Plengkung National Park, on the southern coast of the Blambungan Peninsula, Java.

getting there Fly to Bali, then drive north to Gilamanuk and catch a car ferry to Bangi Wangi in Java. From there drive to Grajagan village, and catch a boat across a huge bay to the break.

perfect day South swell of eight to 10 feet, neap tides, southeast trade winds.

best months May–July.

boards A couple of pintail guns for powerful, hollow surf (you'll probably break at least one).

essentials Sunblock, first-aid kit, booties for long reef walks,

other waves 20/20s and Chickens are smaller, softer sections further down the reef. Tiger Trails is the token right, way down into the bay about half an hour's walk away. These waves have their moments, but they aren't what surfers travel to G-Land for.

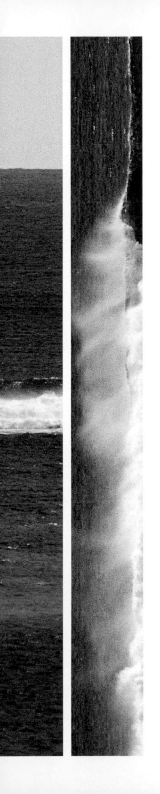

haapiti
moorea
sean doherty

Rising abruptly out of the Pacific, Moorea's lush, green, shark-tooth mountains form surfing's most awe-inspiring backdrop. Sitting in the line-up at Haapiti, gazing back across the lagoon toward the mountains, peacefully drowning in the moment, it's easy to overlook the fact you're actually surfing a world-class lefthander.

Moorea was the inspiration behind James Michener's paradise in *Bali Hai*. Huey designed the heart-shaped island with both surfers and lovers in mind, and we're not just talking about the special kind of love that exists between a man and a barrelling lefthander. A favourite with honeymooners, Moorea is one of the few places in the world where you can successfully merge romance and surfing.

Here, once you've had your daily two-surf allowance, there are plenty of ways to pass the dreaded 'us' time. A trip up to Belvedere lookout on the island's north side will give you a magnificent view of this most magnificent of islands. You can sneak into one of the big resort hotels and sunbake on their chalk-white beaches. You can buy a yellowfin tuna from a roadside fisherman and slice it up back at your digs for some *poisson cru*. The world's best tattooist also lives on the island, so if you want to get your girl's name tattooed across your forehead, or 'Mother' on your biceps, go crazy. And once you've done all that, there's an insane (and for the purposes of this book, nameless) righthander on the other side of the island where your girl can watch you surf into the sunset. Ahhh, romance.

Looking back toward shore from the Haapiti line-up, you'd also be excused for thinking you were at Teahupoo. Fortunately, the left at Haapiti is a bit more forgiving than its cousin across the channel: it breaks best in the same swells as Teahupoo; but while a west swell there makes the place a death zone, the more west in the swell at Haapiti, the better. On the whole, though, it's a great, fun left that holds up to eight feet.

Haapiti is perched on the southern lip of a postcard-perfect reef pass – great news for manufacturers of postcards, but extremely poor news for surfers having to paddle out. The locals aren't too keen on boat operators shuttling guys out to the break, so you're left with few options other than paddle power. The reef pass here is a big one, draining the bright-blue lagoon, so on the outgoing tide of a big swell it becomes a giant, tropical S-bend. Bring a leg-rope made of anchor rope, make sure you start paddling back to shore before you're tired, and if paddling back on the outgoing tide stick to the inside edge of the reef to avoid having to fight the current.

While Moorea might be a great place to take the girl, Haapiti itself probably isn't. I found this out firsthand when my girlfriend Simi, sitting on a kayak in the channel watching me surf, suddenly, despite her best efforts, began drifting off in the general direction of Australia. Former world champ Tom Carroll also found out that Haapiti is not the lefthander of love when he and wife Lisa took a tinnie out to check the break, only for the outboard motor to snap off and sink, and the boat to be washed through the break by an eight-foot set. It might cost you a lot of black pearls to redeem yourself after an experience like that.

And if you thought the current at Haapiti was dangerous, wait until you check your bank statement. For while Moorea is possibly the world's most beautiful island, it is also one of the most expensive. But though most of the accommodation is limited to five-star, luxury hotels, there are some more affordable options for the scumbag travelling surfer and his girl. Yet you know what they say – love don't come cheap – and if you love both your girl and barrelling lefthanders equally, Moorea might be worth six months of fish-fingers and public transport.

haapiti facts

location   Western side of Moorea, French Polynesia, not too far from the Tahitian capital of Papeete.

getting there   Fly to Faa'a airport in Papeete, from where it's a 45-minute ferry over 'the Sea of the Moon' to Moorea, followed by a 15-minute drive to the west side of the island.

the perfect day   Six feet of southwest swell, mid-morning trade winds, a boat ride out there.

best months   April–September.

boards   A shortboard with a bit of extra beef is the go, especially as you may be paddling it more than a kilometre to get out there.

essentials   One girl of your dreams, some basic French (if not Tahitian), some good surf fitness, a strong leg-rope, a fat wallet, and some sunscreen.

accommodation   Mainly five-star resorts, but there are some cheaper options, including a cool 'surf resort' at Haapiti itself.

other waves   There's an amazing, if brutally shallow, righthander on the other side of the island which breaks in east or pure-south swells.

honolua bay
hawaii
sean doherty

On Oahu's North Shore, talk of a 'bay swell' always sets the place abuzz. It just depends which bay you're talking about. For while the rhino-chasing fraternity will be dusting off their Waimea guns, another group of surfers will be making cunning plans to surf a bay of their own. While their big-wave brethren will be taking the drop at giant Waimea, contemplating only survival, these guys will be surfing Honolua Bay contemplating one of the most perfect barrels in the known universe, and a wall imploring you to write on it the story of your life's best wave.

'We were going past Waimea on the way to the airport, and I knew that it took three to four hours for the swell that was hitting Waimea to move on to Honolua,' recalls Rabbit Batholomew, 1978 world champ and a veteran of dozens of Honolua missions. 'I remember saying to my friends, as a 25-foot set went through Waimea, "Watch, we'll be surfing this set at Honolua".'

The Honolua run is a tradition for many surfers camped out on neighbouring Oahu's North Shore. At the first sign of a serious 20-plus-feet-at-20-plus-seconds swell, they'll be on the phone, booking a 20-minute inter-island flight to Maui. They're a strange, clandestine bunch, and only communicate with each other by understated nods and winks. After all, Honolua gets crowded enough with Maui locals, so you don't want to bring any more guys with you than good company demands.

Honolua Bay is one of those waves whose mystique has been forged as much by the rich history of the place as by the magical, rustic quality of the wave itself. Its steep, seamless walls once in the late 60s played host to an evolutionary battle, with Aussies Nat Young and Bob McTavish on their cut-down vee-bottoms up against Gerry Lopez and Reno Abellira on their Brewer mini-guns. The 70s, however, were the heyday of Honolua. Before the crowds, before the surf media had blown it open for the first time, the pineapple fields, ochre soil, and rifling blue tubes were the ultimate escape – even if only from a paddle out at 25-foot Waimea.

'I don't think there's a better bowl in the world to backdoor,' says Aussie surfing legend Terry Fitzgerald. 'You can get in there, comb your hair, have a look around, check it out, listen to the silence, come out, and your hair's still perfectly parted. I'll tell you what, though, it's a runway out there: you can peel off that bowl and some of the cutbacks you can lay down are sensational . . . That's the whole thing about Honolua – what you see is what you get.'

The dirt road into the place is the only remnant of a time when Honolua was a quiet surfing backwater. Today it gets as crowded as the North Shore, and swell-forecasting technology means it's not getting any less when the all-to-rare, big northwest swell conditions come into alignment. Breaking around the high surrounding cliffs that give the place a stadium-like feel, Honolua needs a heap of swell owing to the fact that the neighbouring island of Molokai blocks most of it.

The outside section of Coconuts is quick and heavy, but it's the Cave section that is true Honolua. With enough west in the swell, the wave will just keep horseshoeing through the inside before eventually cannonballing your smiling carcass into the deep waters of the bay itself. Your soul trip may, however, be ruined by being swept into the Cave and dashed against the cliff while you attempt to paddle out, a common occurrence once the swell gets above eight feet. On bigger days the you'll see quite a few guys climbing back up the cliffs with beaten-up boards, and heads that look like mashed pineapples. But one good wave will be enough to time-warp you back to 1975 and have you blissed-out on the Honolua legend.

honolua bay facts

location   Northwest Maui, Hawaii.

getting there   Fly to Honolulu, from where it's a 20-minute flight over to Maui. Conversely, if you choose to paddle it may take you three days.

the perfect day   Eight–10 feet of northwest swell, light easterly trade winds.

best months   November–March.

boards   Nothing too big, as Honolua is predominantly a barrelling wave that also offers scope for some big turns. Pintails between 6'4" and 6'10" will do the trick.

essentials   If you're on Oahu, the ability to know what a good Honolua swell looks like on the charts. If you're on Maui, the patience to wait for one. You'll also need a strong leggie – you don't want to lose your board here.

accommodation   Maui is a popular tourist destination, and there's plenty of affordable accommodation at nearby Lahaina. Try to prebook a car/accommodation package, to save yourself some money.

other waves   Maui's got several other quality reefs, many of which come to life under the same swell as Honolua. On the island's south shore is Maalaea, the quickest (and possibly most inconsistent) wave in the world. If you're really feeling adventurous, Peahi (you might also know it as Jaws) is just around the corner.

hossegor
france
ben mondy

You can thank a little man with serious power issues – and no, we aren't talking about Tom Carroll – for the famed hollow beach breaks that have made Hossegor one of the most alluring surfing spots in the world.

It was in the late 18th century that France's then ruler Napoleon Bonaparte re-routed the River Ardour from its natural entry at Hossegor to Bayonne, about 50 kilometres south. If it wasn't for that rather radical piece of geographical engineering, instead of the current mix of huge lumbering outside peaks, shore-slapping barrels and the myriad, continually disappearing and reappearing rip bowls, there'd be a giant wave-devouring hole as the Ardour poured into the Bay of Biscay.

The first beneficiaries of Napoleon's barrel formation were the local surfers. A local surfing community, led by Biarritz locals George Hennebutte and Joel de Rosnay, quickly sprang up after Hollywood screenwriter Peter Viertel brought surfing to France back in 1956, when he was on the Basque coast filming *The Sun also Rises*. In the late 60s, guys like Billy Hamilton, Wayne Lynch and Nat Young went over to the Bay of Biscay and documented their discoveries in surf flicks. By the 1970s word had spread about the incredible waves and lifestyle in the southwest corner of France. But it was still a relatively close-kept secret until the Junior World Championships were held in Biarritz in 1980. Seventy of the world's best young surfers, plus entourage and surf media, converged on Biarritz; and with excellent waves and a winner by the name of Tom Curren, France was very officially placed on the surfing map.

Years later, Curren returned to marry a French surfer and based himself there. And he wasn't alone. The allure of the French beach breaks, the beautiful women who flock to the white sandy beaches of Hossegor, the cruisy lifestyle and the lack of scrutiny seduced many a surfer – be it world champs or scruffy backpackers – to stay here for long periods. One of the most famous residents was Gary 'Kong' Elkerton. 'I went to France for the 84 world titles and fell in love with the place,' he recalls. 'The best beach breaks in the world, no crowds, and I was young and stoked to be out of Australia. Also there was a girl . . .' Kong moved to France permanently in 1985, and only returned to live in his native Australia 20 years later.

Quite a few expats mirrored this experience, falling in love first with the waves and then usually with a local lass. In the early 80s an expatriate posse that included Aussies Maurice Cole, Stephen Bell and Wayne Lynch were soon joined by the likes of Curren and Robbie Page. Throughout this time the European surf industry was booming, with Quiksilver, Rip Curl and Billabong, among others, all basing their European operations in Biarritz and Hossegor. Meanwhile pro surfing competitions were established; especially in the late 80s, the French leg of the pro tour was seen as the most debauched month of an already debauched surfing calendar. The 90s saw continued growth, in both the local surf scene and the number of visiting surfers. World-class locals also started establishing

Throughout the change from sleepy French surfing town to European hub of all things surfing, the one constant has been the waves.

themselves, culminating in Mikey Picon becoming the first ever French surfer to compete on the World Championship Tour in 2006. In 2007, 19-year-old wunderkid Jeremy Flores also flew the French flag at the elite level.

Throughout the change from sleepy French surfing town to European hub of all things surfing, the one constant has been the waves. The Hossegor beachies, which sit in the last 10 kilometres of a 100-kilometre stretch of straight, sandy beach, are broken into five separate locales, starting with Epi Nord and Le Gravierre, the outside and inside banks respectively that lie in front of the main drag. Epi Nord is capable of holding waves of any size, with local tow-in crews now surfing it regularly around the 20-foot mark. It is Le Gravierre that generally gives Hossegor its reputation: here waves break up to 10 feet, usually about three metres from shore in about a metre and a half of water. Huge cavernous barrels unleash with neck- and board-breaking ferocity, the power a function of the deep water it travels across – the deepest part of the Bay of Biscay, which is directly in front of Hossegor, is around 5000 metres, so the waves arrive on the shallow Le Grav banks pretty much unmolested.

Moving northwards up the stretch, the beach is divided into Estagnots, Bourdaines and Le Penon. All these provide a variety of shifting breaks, with tides and winds and butterfly-wings all changing the nature of the breaks. At low tide, six-foot screamers push across the outside banks, often almost untouchable, but a change in tide can perform miracles, with perfect A-frame peaks zipping off for a few precious hours. It can be really fickle, and a constant stalker-like monitoring of all the banks on all the tides is essential if you want to score in these parts.

So it can be unpredictable, hot and flat, crowded in summer and freezing in winter, and empty beach breaks are definitely a thing of the past. But if you've had the chance to score four hours of perfect sand barrels, chased down by cheap, fine red wine and excellent French cuisine, and maybe, just maybe, a few cold beers in Rockfood nightclub, you'll know why Hossegor is a must-do surf experience. Quite simply, there is nowhere else in the surfing world quite like it.

hossegor facts

location   Hossegor is in the Basque region of southwest France, about 160 kilometres south of Bordeaux.

getting there   International airports at Bordeaux (two hours drive away) and Biarritz (45 minutes away).

the perfect day   A six-foot swell is being brushed by a light easterly offshore and, every 100 metres or so, triangle banks are spitting left and right tubes 15 metres from shore. The hardest part is picking your bank.

best months   September–November. There's a heap of Atlantic swell and plentiful offshore days, and the summer crowds have disappeared.

boards   With the exception of Epi Nord, where Sunset-style guns are needed, the short, sharp beach barrels only need your standard shortboard — just have a few, as snappages are very common.

essentials   A wardrobe of rubber. You'll need a springsuit for summer, a 3/2 for autumn, and booties and a serious 4/3 for winter.

accommodation   Choose from well-equipped camping grounds, hotels and holiday apartments, though accommodation is very scarce in the August (summer) holidays.

other waves   Take your pick — less crowded beach-break heaven for two hours in both directions, while Mundaka is a two-hour bolt south into Spain.

jeffrey's bay
south africa
craig jarvis

It's a cliché to call J-Bay a Mecca for surfers the world over, but it is a place that any surfer, pilgrim or not, has a need to see. A natural phenomenon, J-Bay has held the surfing world in awe ever since it was discovered back in 1959 by legendary South African pioneer surfer John Whitmore, though it was only surfed a few years later.

There are many stories about who were the first surfers to paddle out at J-Bay. Some rumours tend towards the Australian duo who pioneered the break wearing tennis shoes to protect themselves from the rocks – Morris and the Beast, they were called, or something like that. The general consensus, however, is that a bunch of Cape Town surfers headed by Gus Gobel and Brian McLarty were the first to give it a go. They tried to surf Supertubes, the centrepiece of the wave here, but found it too fast and ended up hanging at the Point, a much softer and more user-friendly section.

There are also a number of legends about how Jeffrey's Bay got its name, but we're going to stick to local hotel-owner and whaler J. A. Jeffrey, who ran a hotel here in the 19th century. As a town, Jeffrey's Bay has gone through a huge metamorphosis, with rampant, unchecked development being the norm over the last 20 years. The result is that those who had Supers-facing property are now multi-millionaires, and everyone else is scratching to buy land on the hill. Ugly and disjointed, the development has not affected the perfect waves, thank God. You only need to look at Bruce's Beauties, just around the corner, to find one of the best waves in the world destroyed by the stabilising of the dunes for development.

Jeffrey's Bay is Billabong country, and the head office, led by Cheron Kraak, is situated at the southern end of the town, along with surf shops, factory shops, skate parks and restaurants. Quiksilver and Rip Curl are also in town. Billabong runs the Billabong J-Bay World Championship Tour every year, and it is one of the most popular WCT contests. With a 12-day waiting period, it always seems to score sick waves, sometimes at the very end of the event.

The wave itself is a ridiculously long righthand point break, with a number of particular sections. At the top of the point is Boneyards, the precursor to Supertubes and a good wave itself in certain conditions. Then there is Supers, a long, barrelling righthander that is quite mesmerising in its length and levels of perfection. The end section, called Impossibles, leads into Tubes, a short, barrelling section which leads into the Point. It is the understated goal of anyone surfing J-Bay to make a wave from the tip of Boneyards all the way to the Point. It has been done before, apparently, but not by this scribe – who, in fact, after a couple of trips there every year over the last 20 years, has never seen anyone make it all the way through. Those who do can be very proud of themselves.

Jeffrey's Bay was home for a few years to Australian journalist Derek Hynd, who purchased land and built on a prime spot in front of the gully at Supers. Mickey Dora also called J-Bay home during his final years. The crowds get out of control at times, and the localism gets pretty heavy as well. But when a good swell comes to town and sticks around for a while, as it sometimes does, the crowds get a bit thinner and everyone gets a couple of waves.

jeffrey's bay facts

location   About 70 km west of Port Elizabeth, off the Garden Route.

getting there   Fly to Port Elizabeth, or take the mellow Garden Route drive up from Cape Town.

the perfect day   Six-foot southwest swell, light southwest winds, low tides at midday, and a big Springbok rugby game on (which means no one in the water).

best months   May–September, though the area can and does get epic at any time of the year. It can also go flat for months.

boards   It's a fast wave and there is a lot of paddling, so an average surfer would do well to go a couple of inches longer at J-Bay. The pros, however, ride shortboards in the contests because the wave is ultimately a hotdog.

essentials   A good wetsuit: it gets cold in winter and the wind is freezing. A 4/3 is necessary, and maybe some booties, even a hood. Summer is pretty balmy and sometimes it even gets warm enough for boardies.

accommodation   Most types, from budget to five-star.

other waves   There are heaps in the area, though they all get overlooked relative to Supers. Seal Point and the aforementioned Bruce's are two other good pointbreaks, and there are some sick beachies around.

joaquina
brazil
matt griggs

On the ocean side of the beautiful, rich and cosmopolitan island city of Florianopolis, Joaquina provides some of the best waves and best surfers Brazil has to offer. The home of the Padaratz brothers, Flavio and Neco (the most successful of all Brazil's professionals), it is also home to the Nova Schin Pro (Brazil's only World Championship Tour event), and the Onbongo Pro (a six-star World Qualifying Series) the week before. The reason for this isn't just its consistency, the wedgy lefts that run down the long sandy Joaquina beach, or the variety of beach breaks that span picturesque Florianopolis, including nearby Praia Mole and Mozambique. I won't waste any more time detailing waves you could catch at any summer beach anywhere around the world, but get to the real reason you are going: chicks!

It's true what they say about the female population here greatly outnumbering males. It's true what they say about every single girl wearing a G-string, and that every girl is fit and healthy and beautiful in that special Latino way. It's also true that when you walk down the beach in your boardshorts, towards the summery beach breaks and below the massive sand dunes that feed the endless banks below the green Amazon-like forest, you'll be struggling to find some spare sand to walk on – not that you'll be looking at the sand.

The waves here can get fun. They can actually get really fun. But there are no reef breaks with ledge barrels, no long point breaks to really draw out your surfing – and no bombies to get some shots away on your gun. You could bring one board here: one that goes in two-foot beach breaks.

If you get bored by the waves, or somebody's dad is after you, you can always drive south towards Imbituba for a little escape. It's a Narrabeen-like left/right fixed bank that lays claim to being one of Brazil's best waves; the WCT event has been held here for the last three years. It's a beautiful coastline with offshore islands and an aesthetic hinterland. But it's become a bit of a ghost town since the 1990s collapse of the coal-mining industry on which Imbituba port depended, leaving a dusty little town trying to regain its identity with the ocean. It is a quality wave but, like most in Brazil, a little weak.

There are also some waves at Garopaba and many other beaches on that strip of coast. You'll have to battle the odd muddy track to get to some of them. If it's been raining, perhaps you won't even get there without a 4WD. But you now what? After a session or two there, you'll once again realise the real reason you are here in Brazil – and it's not to surf perfect waves. The answer to that riddle is on an island called Florianopolis. If you want to find some perfect waves, get barrelled in tropical waters with nobody around, I suggest you go somewhere else.

joaquina facts

location   Around 100 km south of Rio de Janeiro.

getting there   Fly to either Rio or Sao Paulo, from where it's a short flight or a long drive.

the perfect day   Sunny and crowded. Preferably a weekend or public holiday.

best months   January and February, during Carnival.

boards   Shortboard. You could get away with one board here, as the wave won't break and the wave won't get over six feet, not with any power anyway.

essentials   Sunscreen, grovel board, mirrored sunglasses.

accommodation   There are three hotels on Joaquina and one big one around the corner at Praia Mole. Town is a short drive away.

other waves   Praia Mole and Mozambique are good back-up waves, but Joaquina is the best.

kirra
australia
sean doherty

Kirra never was a place of pilgrimage. 'Pilgrimage' implies that you will, at some stage, actually go home. Over the past three decades, many of the guys who've cruised up the coast to catch a cyclone swell at Kirra have never returned. One good barrel at Kirra is a portal to a dimension where your past life ceases to have meaning, and dwelling on the memory will induce a glazed, distant stare. Yes, this is – or more to the point *was* – quite a wave.

Long regarded as the best wave not only in Australia but in the world, there was a time when Kirra was almost considered unsurfable. Guys on clunky, pedestrian longboards simply couldn't match it for toe. It wasn't until surfboards shrank and local guys started exploring the innermost reaches of the barrel that they truly realised the gold mine (more aptly, the sand mine) they were sitting on. It's little surprise that riding deep tubes was pioneered here in the 70s, by the likes of Rabbit Bartholomew, Peter Townend and the greatest of them all, the legendary Michael Peterson. Other names synonymous with Kirra include Betsy, Bola, Roger, Dinah – not surfers, but tropical cyclones that have spawned landmark Kirra swells.

True Kirra comes to life under the brutal caress of a long-fetch easterly or north-east cyclone swell. Standing up just off Big Groyne, the famous righthander begins its mercurial run down the point – zipping along a near-dry sandbank, this is a start-to-finish, gurgling, green sand-barrel with reef-break intensity. As the wave spits you out of one barrel section, it will often drop you down a step into an even deeper, submarine one, and may do so three or four times on a single wave. So abrupt is the sandbank, and so focused the energy, that three-foot waves will become stand-up pits, throwing out three times their height. The wave will often dredge so much sand off the bottom that the lip gets a concrete-like consistency, and has the propensity to both atomise surfboards and grind surfers into the bank like sidewalk roaches.

'All we depend on for quality surf in Queensland is the sand,' declared Michael Peterson in a letter to *Tracks* magazine in 1975, shortly after Kirra's famous rock groynes were first bulldozed into place. 'It has to be in the right places at the right times. If we don't get the sand we don't get the waves.' Kirra's sand has been in a state of constant flux since time immemorial, and the bickering about where exactly the 'right' place is and how to achieve it has resulted in Kirra witnessing more sand battles than Rommel. The original groynes, despite the protests of surfers at the time, helped stabilise the beach and eventually even improved the wave. But the Kirra of 1975 is largely unrecognisable in the Kirra of today.

It's as if there's only a finite amount of surfing magic shared between Kirra and its neighbouring point breaks of Snapper and Greenmount, so by pumping the sand to create the Superbank they've just robbed Peter to pay Paul. Today Kirra is being buried alive under the same suffocating blanket of sand that brought the Superbank to life – where there was once virtually no beach, it now looks like the Sahara. The whole bay outside Kirra has also got progressively shallower, taking much of the gumption out of the swell as it marches in. So much sand has filled the bay that the wave no longer follows the contour of the original point and has fundamentally

This is a start-to-finish, gurgling, green sand barrel with reef-break intensity.

changed – it's almost become too fast to ride and, as a result, classic Kirra days have been few and far between in the past five years.

The Superbank, while technically perfect, is still a prefab construction, just like the pastel-coloured concrete units that tower over it. Kirra, on the other hand, has a life-force all of its own, and it's this soul that locals are hoping will prevail. The fickle nature of the sand flow here means it's only one good cyclone away from returning to its natural formation, and locals who surfed Kirra in her prime are all living in hope.

kirra facts

location   On the southern Gold Coast, Queensland, about 100 km south of Brisbane.

getting there   Fly to Coolangatta (about a two-minute drive away, but you can walk if you have to). Or fly to Brisbane from where it's around one hour away by bus or car.

the perfect day   Four to six feet of east-northeast swell courtesy of a long fetch from a cyclone sitting south of Vanuatu. Light winds from the southwest. This day, however, is more likely to have occurred in 1977 than in 2007.

best months   January–May, when northerly swells prevail while northerly winds have backed away.

boards   The quickest shortboard you've got, something with some drive. Then bring a spare.

essentials   Paddling stamina, patience to deal with the madding crowd, a beaten-up old Mitsubishi Lancer with four friends to keep you company on the drive up the coast.

accommodation   Plenty of tourist accommodation in both Kirra and neighbouring Coolangatta.

other waves   If you're sick of getting barrelled at Kirra, take a walk up the beach and get barrelled on the Superbank instead.

la jolla
mexico
sean doherty

Taj Burrow's eyes were still spinning in their sockets like a poker machine. 'It's the best wave I've ever surfed. Full stop. It really is. I've never surfed a wave that perfect in my life. Guaranteed.'

Twenty seconds of tube time on the one wave has a tendency to regress grown men into stammering, surf-stoked grommets, and that's exactly what the rifling righthand pits of La Jolla had just done to Burrow. Similarly, many of his pro surfing comrades developed temporary tics when asked to describe the waves they had just scored in a remote, dusty corner of Mexico. 'It's a cross between Kirra and Burleigh, but it's better than both of them,' said an incredulous Bede Durbidge.

And for two weeks in June 2006, during the Rip Curl Pro Search event at La Jolla, that's exactly what the world's best surfers enjoyed. The formerly underground Mexican point break played host to a leg of the World Championship Tour, and produced what was unanimously regarded as some of the greatest waves seen in 30 years of professional surfing. The surfing gringos had lucked on a once-in-a-decade swell, and the chocolate tubes were simply hypnotic. The sand on the point, groomed by recent heavy rainfall that had flushed out local waterways, was perfect to a grain. The big southerly swell stormed out of the Pacific and wrapped in behind the point at La Jolla, before firing off mindless perfection for hundreds of metres. Surfing the place became a case of speed management. The bottom-turn-kickstall-five-second-barrel routine was replayed over and over, often several times on the same wave. At the end of the week the guys packed their bags for the next tour event, at Jeffrey's Bay, with heavy hearts – it's not often you travel to the world's best righthand point anticipating a substantial drop in wave quality.

The reality of the situation is that La Jolla – Spanish for 'the jewel' – isn't even La Jolla. The righthander was code-named in an attempt to throw people off its true location, an effort that proved futile once the first perfect barrels of the event were webcast to millions around the world. For decades the place held semi-secret status, existing only as a late-night, whiskey-breath whisper from the mouths of a

This wave was code-named La Jolla in an attempt to throw people off its true location, which proved futile once the perfect barrels were webcast around the world.

select crew who had surfed the famous barrels of Puerto Escondido and figured there had to be more waves to the south.

For most of the year, however, the Jewel is closer to a cubic zirconia. The point itself has a very narrow swell window, and needs a big south or southeast swell to even begin to show signs of life. It's stiflingly hot and often crowded, the mozzies will take your arm, and your feeble western digestive system will have trouble adapting to the local cuisine. The tiny pueblo in front of the wave is poky, dusty, isolated – and not at all prepared for the surfing onslaught that would follow in the slipstream of the 2006 contest.

The Rip Curl event was the modern global surfing machine bivouacked in a sleepy surfing backwater. More puritanical members of the surfing brotherhood have devoted page after page on chatrooms not

only about how the event broke surfing's golden rule of not exposing secret spots, but also about the imperialist nature of dropping the event into a third-world village like La Jolla. There have even been rumours of offers by an unnamed surf company, to buy the entire town.

One thing is for sure – La Jolla will never be the same again, and let's hope that those trawling atlases and internet sites to find its true location treat the place and the people with respect when they eventually find it. 'Surfers are the biggest kooks,' said one chatroom posting, lamenting the loss of yet another secret spot in an ever-shrinking world. 'We are our own worst enemy.'

la jolla facts

location   Oaxaca, southeastern Mexico.

getting there   Fly into Huatulco, which is around 600 km southeast of Mexico City, then head south. That's all we're giving you.

the perfect day   Five feet of southeast swell, light northerly winds.

best months   December–February, the southern-hemisphere winter.

boards   A few good shortboards built for speed, as you're likely to snap one or two if the place gets a swell. If you've got something with channels, this wave is perfect for it.

essentials   A spare everything – leggies, fins, ding kits – as surfing supplies are thin on the ground. Bug spray, sunscreen, and plenty of bottled drinking water.

accommodation   There is plenty of cheap accommodation in the nearby major town.

other waves   Yes: it turns out that La Jolla isn't the only jewel in this neck of the woods.

lagundri bay
nias island
sean doherty

Equal parts myth, magic and malaria, the righthander at Indonesia's Lagundri Bay is something more than simply a perfect wave. For 20 years the milky green barrels of the Point – framed and famed by the banks of palm trees across the bay – *was* the surfing dream.

The discovery of Lagundri Bay in 1975 by a trio of intrepid young Aussie surfers has become the stuff of surfing legend. Twenty-year-old Kevin Lovett and his mate Jon Giesel, 22, were on a trip of spiritual discovery through Asia, and it was only a piece of sacred serendipity that they stumbled across the wave that would soon become a brother to them.

In a village on the shores of Sumatra's Lake Toba, they noticed that the chief of the local Batak village had a map on the wall of his losmen, highlighting the island of Nias. Feeling drawn to the place by some otherworldly force, they were joined on the ferry across the Mentawai Strait by soon-to-be-legendary Aussie surf pioneer, Peter Troy. A week later, on pushbike, the three emerged from a clearing onto a long white beach and it was then they saw it – a flawless righthander they immediately swore a blood oath to keep secret (later, Lovett even flipped all his photos of the wave to make it appear to be a left).

But while they appeared to have discovered paradise, they were soon to find out that it came at a price. The people of Nias have maintained their age-old culture, and Lovett and Giesel were unknowingly being sized up by the local *emali* (village headhunters, who, according to legend could shape-shift, turn into animals, and exist in nine places at once). Sharing a couple of spliffs with the head magician saved their necks, however, and they continued to surf their new discovery for weeks with ne'er a care in the world. Or so they thought. Six months later Giesel, who'd contracted malaria while camping at the point, died from double pneumonia. But in the three decades since Lagundri was first stumbled upon, the trek has become a surfing rite of passage.

Located on the southwestern tip of Nias, the mouth of Lagundri Bay faces directly into the prevailing Indian Ocean swell. The Point is a lava shelf on the inside of the bay, breaking directly in front of the Sorake Beach village that has sprung up to cater for surf tourists chasing the dream. From the dry-hair paddle-out in the Keyhole, to the kick-out into the safe, jade-coloured waters of the channel, the place is pure magic when it's on. Take the drop, set a rail, and wait for your seven seconds of joy. Apart from an hour or so of cross-shore 'church wind' (which blows from across the bay from the direction of a large church on the hill), the place stays offshore and clean as a whistle all day.

But as it has done in many places, the flood of western surfers has corrupted the Lagundri dream. The occasional rip-off, unscrupulous business practice, and bad vibing of visiting surfers have been by-products of a lucrative local economy that has sprung up around surfing. On the upside, it has also spawned two generations of hot local surfers. And while the surf-charter industry booms around Nias and the adjacent Mentawais, it has had little impact on the numbers in the water at Lagundri, owing to the big harbour fee imposed on visiting boats.

The 2004 Boxing Day tsunami temporarily flooded Sorake Beach village, but the earthquake in March 2005 produced another tsunami that was far more devastating, with infrastructure damaged and houses destroyed. Even the wave itself was radically altered, the ocean floor under the Point being raised by close to a metre, meaning the famous almond-eye barrels are now a little rounder and heavier. For surfers at least, the dream, by all reports, just got better.

lagundri bay facts

location   Nias Island, about 125 km off the western coast of Sumatra, Indonesia.

getting there   A total mission. Unless you're going overland (a total, *total* mission), fly into Medan. Flights to Nias from Medan are rare, and sketchy when they do take off. The only other option for the travelling surfer is the Sibolga ferry from Sumatra. (Tip: Sleep with your boards close by, in case you wake up with the cabin half filled with water.)

the perfect day   Eight feet of southwest swell combed by a northeasterly trade wind.

best months   April–September, when winter swells storm out of the Indian Ocean and the local dry season ensures that the wind swings mechanically offshore.

boards   Take two boards more than you think you need, as surfboard retailers are thin on the ground, and the place has a habit of snapping boards. Start with your standard shortboard and work up to a 6'8" or 6'10".

essentials   A good round of shots from your doctor, some doxycycline for malaria, a bucket of sunscreen and a back-up set of every bit of surf hardware (leggies, fins, etc.). Plus a good set of cards in case you encounter a two-week flat spell.

accommodation   There's a bunch of losmens looking straight out over the bay, which can be rented cheaply. Uni's Losmens, run by the local Mr Fixit, will give you a roof over your head and your boards fixed for not much.

other waves   Indicators, outside the Point, is a barely makeable right surfed by people who don't like skin. The island has plenty of other waves: the challenge is to find them and then get there.

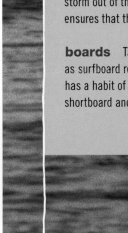

lance's right
mentawai islands
sean doherty

It's every surfer's dream to discover a perfect wave, and then have it named in their honour. Very few get to live this dream, and even fewer still get to have their name become, in surfing folklore, synonymous with one of the most beautiful waves in the world. Lance Knight is one such gentleman.

Lance's story begins on 18 March 1991, when the young Aussie surfer from Yamba stumbled up the beach and into the village of Katiet on the island of Sipora. Lance was 'land-crabbing' (as the practice has become known) – living with the locals for months on end in the Indo jungle, risking malaria – all to score filthy surf. And score filthy surf he did. The righthander in front of Katiet just happens to be one of the world's best waves; it was just that no one, apart from Lance, knew it at the time.

Fast forward to today and things are a little different. Within five years of Lance's find, the secret leaked out and the place exploded. The whole Mentawai island chain and its surfing treasures captured the imagination of the surfing world, and there are now 40-plus charter boats working the islands. The Mentawai boat trip has become the ultimate in surfing hedonism: first-world comfort in a third-world surfing paradise.

It's easy to see why surfers have been hypnotised by this place. The Mentawais are a labyrinth of pristine tropical islands around

The Mentawais are a labyrinth of pristine tropical islands around which the prevailing southwest swells push into some of the most geometrically sublime reefs in the known surfing world.

which the prevailing southwest swells push into some of the most geometrically sublime reefs in the known surfing world. The islands are home to more than 20 world-class waves, and there are another 20 that aren't far behind. The equatorial doldrums ensure that most days the water is like sheet glass. The waves don't have the brutishness of places like Hawaii or Tahiti, and the water is bathtub-warm. Sound good?

Lance's Right (formerly and still also known as Hollow Trees) is generally the first port of call for surf charter boats after an overnight sail across the Sumatran Strait from Padang. It's day one of your charter, and as the break materialises in the early morning light, the froth on board among your surfing mates is as palpable as the thick tropical air. From behind the break you see a set spinning off down the reef, framed by the ubiquitous coconut palms and white-sand beach. The keener of your crew will have already waxed up and bailed into the line-up as the boat manoeuvres to anchor in the channel. Your first wave should be enough to reassure you that you made the right decision spending five grand on this trip instead of buying the plasma TV.

As far as righthand barrels go, Lance's Right has few peers. It's a start-to-finish, five-star drainpipe, breaking hard over a sharp limestone and coral shelf. The wave is fun up to six feet, but then starts to get serious, capping on an outside

bombie before turning itself inside out on the reef proper. Follow one too closely to the inside of the reef and you may find yourself laid out on the Surgeon's Table (in case you're wondering: no, this isn't a good thing). Like all waves in the Mentawais, Lance's can be moody as subtle shifts in winds, tides and swell – not to mention the frequent rain squalls – can all conspire to change the wave's complexion a dozen times during any given day.

The only catch here is the crowds. With up to half a dozen boats moored in the channel at any one time, the line-up can get busy. This is accentuated by the fact that the swells are generally all long-fetch, and often there'll be long lulls in between sets. Of course, herein lies the beauty of the Mentawai boat trip – you can always up anchor and sail off into the sunset to another perfect wave.

lance's right facts

location   Sipora Island, about 100 km west of Sumatra, Mentawai Islands, Indonesia.

getting there   A flight to either Singapore or Denpasar, then a connection to the West Sumatran capital of Padang. This is followed by an overnight sail on a charter boat. There are also flights to the neighbouring island of Siberut, from where you'll require boat transfers.

the perfect day   Six-to-eight feet of southwest swell, a light offshore wind.

best months   The local dry season, April–September.

boards   Your typical Indo boards will do the trick – a couple of inches longer than your usual shortboard, with a touch more volume. Depending on the swell, something between 6'3" and 6'8" will get you out of trouble.

essentials   Industrial-strength sunscreen, a nose for a tube, and a camera to record the wave of your life.

accommodation   Generally below deck on a surf charter boat, although there is also now a land camp at Katiet.

other waves   They're all over the place. Around the western side of Sipora, just a short sail away, is Lance's Left (yes, he found that one too), and Macaronis is about a four-hour sail. They're just the tip of the iceberg.

lennox head
australia
sean doherty

It's little coincidence that the population of Lennox Head is currently listed as 1973. Most of the residents of the small rural town would be happy for Lennox to remain just as it was in that year. The original home of country soul and the endless righthander, this land of milk and honey was first tasted by a pair of Kiwis back in the early 60s. In those days it literally was the land of milk and honey, as the headland at Lennox was still a working dairy farm.

Once word got out, surfers flocked to the place and were soon dodging cowpat landmines on their way through the paddocks out to the point. Lester Brien reported in the October 1970 issue of *Tracks* that the farmer who owned the land on the point had strung barbed wire across the access track, meaning surfers had to do the death shuffle across the notorious Lennox boulders to reach the jump-off spot.

In the early 70s, Lennox was the scene for experimentation of various kinds. Bob McTavish had settled in the area, and was in the process of transforming the longboard into the shortboard. Meanwhile, savant film-maker George Greenough used Lennox as his studio while filming *The Innermost Limits of Pure Fun*. His goal? To film the barrel from the inside out, the authentic surfer's-eye view. 'It was Lennox Head around 1970,' recalls George, 'and I remember being determined to get footage of the wave from inside the tube. I rode the mat, as I knew the spoon wouldn't be buoyant enough to get me into the waves, and I had this military rig 35-mm camera strapped to my back when I paddled out at half-light that morning. I've never seen a swell like it – 18 to 20 seconds, and really thick and heavy. The waves had no entry point, because they were so steep and there was so much water running up the face. I realised the waves breaking way outside weren't as steep, and I ended up 100 metres beyond the normal take-off spot. The third wave in the set looked like the hero wave and I switched on the camera as soon as I took off. I had a ton of speed and the mat was on the edge of its performance capacity. The barrel was throwing easily as high as it was wide and the whole thing had that Rick Griffin cartoon look. It's hard to say how long I travelled in there. I totally forgot about the camera, but when I checked it later I'd used 40 metres of 35-mm film.'

Being dragged kicking and screaming into the 21st century, Lennox has changed remarkably in the past few years. With Byron Bay (just up the road) now another Bondi, those chasing the *real* country are flocking to Lennox and farmland is being subdivided. But while the town itself is changing, the magic of the point remains as it ever was. The coast road snakes around the headland, offering an uninterrupted view – if you're lucky – of clean lines sweeping down the point and into the bay for hundreds of metres. With a strong southeast swell surging around the point and a light southwest wind to groom it, there are fewer finer sights in surfing. Lennox can also handle some real size, and locals will tell you of rideable 15-foot days – just after they've told you the place is full of sharks and a certain death trap. The real danger at, Lennox, though is getting in and out of the water. With the point lined by giant, slippery black boulders, the carnage rate on a six-foot day is roughly one in three.

lennox head facts

location   Far northern New South Wales, 210 km south of Brisbane or 120 km south of the Gold Coast.

getting there   Fly to Coolangatta, from where it is a two-hour drive.

the perfect day   Eight feet of clean southeast swell, light southwest wind

best months   February–September. Even though it prefers swell with some south in it, the point also holds easterly and even northeasterly cyclone swells under the right conditions.

boards   Your normal shortboard will do, but as Lennox can handle 10 feet plus, you don't want a 6'2" to be your only board in case this should happen.

essentials   A laidback vibe, an ego that will withstand being rolled along the rocks while trying to jump off, in full view of the locals.

accommodation   Despite the mushrooming number of high-tariff holiday units, there are still plenty of cheaper options for frugal travellers.

other waves   Head south and you'll find the classy waves of Boulders and Flat Rock. Head north and you'll find Broken Head and the Pass at Byron Bay. Some extra driving time in either direction will take you to Angourie (south) and Kirra (north).

macaronis
mentawai islands
sean doherty

Named after the staple diet of the first guys to camp and surf here, Macaronis has, with good reason, been described as the most-fun wave in the world. Located in Indonesia's Mentawai island group, an area littered with world-class waves, this lefthander is about as good as it gets.

It's obvious why they call these the Sinking Islands. The grey ghosts of once-proud, old-growth trees stand as sentinels over the break at Macaronis, testament to a creeping ocean. Perched on the edge of the Sumatran tectonic plate, the whole island chain is gradually sinking into the ocean at the rate of 2.5 centimetres a year. While this is slowly turning the peninsula behind Macaronis into a giant mangrove swamp, the wave has largely escaped unscathed thanks to the slow taper and perfect shape of its limestone reef.

As to who was first to surf 'Maccas', well, it may depend on who you talk to, for there are a couple of stories in circulation. The most reliable suggests it was Aussie brothers Marty and Danny Madre, in the early 90s. In the years that followed, there was a secret sect of boat operators who knew of the place and would sail in, surf it and then stealthily sail out again. They were sworn to secrecy, but a place this good was never going to stay a secret forever. When word got out in the mid-90s all hell broke loose, and by the end of that decade it was the most photographed wave in the world.

You can see the swells wrap their way down the outside indicator reefs before they finally wrap into the bay and Maccas itself. The wave stands up on the outside ledge and that's where the fun starts. From here it's a magic canvas – if you want to get barrelled, just pull in. Want to throw some big turns? No worries. The wave wraps around the lava reef for 200 metres, and the uniformity of the reef means it never closes out – the best inside section of any wave in the world. Relentlessly steep, it just keeps walling up in front of you asking – nay, demanding – to be hit. More often than not, the wind is breathless and the waves oily-smooth. Macaronis turns into a serious wave at five to six feet, but won't handle much more before it starts washing wide of the reef.

There are only two ways to get out there and surf Macaronis. The first, and most popular, is by charter boat. Up to 40 boats (of varying degrees of seaworthiness) ply their trade out of Padang on the Sumatran mainland, sailing through the Mentawai chain. Pretty well every one of them will stop at Maccas at some stage of each 12-day charter. The journey gives you the freedom to travel to other breaks (and there are plenty), and also means that malaria isn't a problem (the anopheles mosquito can only travel 50 metres over the ocean, and the boats measure out their anchorages accordingly). The boat trip is, however, expensive, the price depending on whether you're taking your chances in the diesel-fumed hold of a fishing boat, or skolling Bintang beers on a scaled-down version of the *Queen Mary*. In 2005 a land camp opened up inside the bay at Macaronis, giving surfers another option.

Unfortunately, the wave's playful reputation makes it a magnet for surfers from around the world, and it can get busy. Really busy. The irony isn't hard to see – you're a million miles from nowhere, surfing a wave with a crowd bigger than the crowd you've left at home. Still, taking off on a set wave here and looking at 100 metres of wall lining up in front of you, you'll soon know why you've made the trek.

macaronis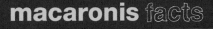

location   North Pagai, about 90 km southwest of Sumatra, Mentawai Islands, Indonesia.

getting there   Generally a flight to either Singapore or Denpasar, followed by a connection to Padang. From there it's an overnight sail on a charter boat.

the perfect day   Five feet of southwest swell, no wind, 20 charter boats surfing near Lance's Right, leaving Macaronis to just you and four mates.

best months   The local dry season, April–September.

boards   Your standard shortboards will do the trick nicely. You'll need a few of them, though.

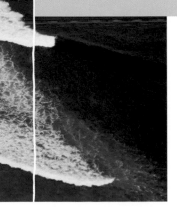

essentials   Even on the boats some surfers still take some form of malaria prevention. Also take 300-plus sunscreen, a good medical kit including plenty of stuff to deal with reef cuts (try the Chinese Tieh Ta Yao Gin), a good camera.

accommodation   Either below deck on a charter boat, inside a losmen at Macaronis Resort, or sharing a tent with 3000 malaria mosquitoes.

other waves   Take your pick. The Mentawais is all world-class waves. For the natural-footer, Lance's Right (the chain's best right) is an hour's speedboat ride away. Green Bush, a far more challenging left, is just around the corner.

margaret river
australia
kirk owers

Australia's southwest is riddled with quality surf. A 120-kilometre wedge of Western Australian coast between Cape Naturaliste and Cape Leeuwin offers more than 20 class waves – most of them reef breaks, all of them powerful. Margies, as Margaret River is known locally, is the most famous on the strip: it's raw, challenging (and occasionally seriously scary), typical of the waves on this bit of the coast.

A former dairy-farming region, Margaret River is now a tourist hub. The coastal highway winds through towering karri eucalypt forests, past dozens of boutique wineries and eye-catching natural attractions. Along the shore, rugged limestone cliffs crumble into the ocean where barely submerged reefs sculpt swell lines into urgent blue cylinders. The profusion of brawny waves in such a small area warrants comparisons with Hawaii's famed North Shore.

Margaret River's main break surges to life on a slanting bed of limestone reef roughly 150 metres from the shore. Its shifty, vertiginous peaks maximise any available swell, and improve with size. Under six feet the peak is split left and right; any bigger, and the right becomes a shorter and increasingly risky option. Margies comes into its own at around eight feet and can handle waves twice that size.

Lack of swell is rarely a problem for Australia's southwest. Storm swells generated far out to sea – the notorious 'Roaring 40s' – regularly smash into the coastline and the Margaret River peak has a habit of catching the unwary. Locals favour thickly glassed Hawaiian-style shooters and heavy-duty leashes, and keep their eyes on the horizon. It's not unusual to hear the pinging of snapped leggies and the groans that follow a broken board when a big set thunders through. A deep-water channel provides easy access and prevents the wave from closing out. Because it's not as hazardous as many of its neighbours, you get all sorts out at Margies even on a solid day. As a result you see some mediocre surfing: the survival crouch, the grim-faced shoulder hop, the overly cautious race to the channel. It can be a heavy wave, but it's not exclusively for experts. If you catch the biggest wave of your life at Margaret River, you will be one of thousands.

The area's best young surfers tend to favour the shorter, faster, hollower waves nearby, leaving Margies for the older locals and tourist hordes. In some respects Margies could be considered a 1980s wave, its lumbering peaks and wide-open walls best suited to old-school, rail-to-rail surfing. For this reason, and because it's a difficult wave to photograph, it hasn't received nearly the amount of magazine and video coverage of nearby waves like North Point. Some of the most legendary Margaret River sessions occurred during the late 80s and early 90s, when it was a regular stop on the Association of Surfing Professionals tour. To surf Margies well, you need to be able to match power with power, and the best surfers here (Tom Carroll, Mark Occhilupo, Dave Macaulay and Mitch Thorson) utilise a driving bottom turn and gouge tight in the pocket or else shoot through tight, collapsing, high-line barrels. Done well, it's a beautiful sight.

Across the channel a ridiculously shallow slab of reef known as the Box offers unnaturally square barrels for the adrenaline seeker. Nearby 'Suicides' (Southside) and the Bombie are good options when Margies is crowded or massive.

To surf Margaret River on your Wild West pilgrimage is a must; to surf it well is the challenge.

margaret river facts

location   290 km south of Perth, Western Australia.

getting there   Fly to Perth and rent a car for the three-hour drive.

the perfect day   Eight feet, long-fetch southwest swell, sunny and offshore. The wind swings onshore early, so don't muck around.

best months   March–May for consistent swell and offshores. Winter gets cold and stormy, but the good days are less crowded. Spring (September–November) can also be good.

boards   As many as you can carry. You'll need your regular shortboard, a mid-sized gun and a 7'-plus shooter if you want to charge the big days. Expect to break a few.

accommodation   Lots, from budget to five-star.

other waves   The Margaret River tourist centre supplies a map showing most surf breaks. Further north, the Gracetown and Yallingup areas also have some superb waves.

essentials   A good wetsuit (err on the side of more rubber than less), and a good surf wagon as the surrounding coast is littered with quality waves. A local contact here is also invaluable, as this good surf can often be tricky to find amongst the raw wind and swell.

mundaka
spain
ben mondy

It's said that you don't know what you've got till it's gone. And never has that been more apt then in 2005, when it was feared that Mundaka, the Spanish river-mouth left, universally regarded as one of the best sandbottom waves in the world, had disappeared off the face of the Earth.

And it wasn't just surfers who lamented the loss of the wave. The whole township of Mundaka, a picturesque Basque village nestled at the edge of the Oka River, suddenly realised that the break – and the surfers that come from all corners of the globe to sample it – was their economic lifeblood. Craig Sage, an Australian who settled in Mundaka in the early 80s and runs a local surf shop, perhaps put it best when he said, 'Mundaka is the symbol of surfing in Europe. If we lose it, it will be like losing part of our soul.'

That year Mundaka also lost the Billabong Pro, the World Championship Tour event that had been held there since 1999 and further cemented Mundaka's place in surfing folklore. Billabong's announcement that the sandbank – which every winter for over 30 years had supplied 400-metre-long freight-train tubes of mind-bending quality – was ruined sent shockwaves around the world. It was akin to hearing that terrorists had stolen the reef at Bells, or that the coral at Teahupoo had suddenly dropped 10 metres. Theories abounded as to the reason for the demise of the sandbank. Most surfers blamed a dredging scheme four kilometres upriver for the absence of a surfable wave on the bank for more than 12 months.

All the protests, laments, and even Spanish government comment, ceased, however, when in April 2006 a huge swell battered the Basque coast and, for a select group of local surfers, Mundaka provided some of the longest, hollowest and best waves in a very, very long time. The break's official reincarnation was settled five months later when a spanking-new, 10-foot northwest swell arrived, with a perfect low tide at midday, powdery blue skies and a perfect offshore wind. It helped that only two hours drive north, a lay-day had been called at the elite Quiksilver Pro in Hossegor, meaning that 45 of the world's best surfers and its best photographers were on hand to tackle and capture the moment. And they weren't disappointed. Occy described that day as, 'one of the top five surfs of my life', while world number six, Joel Parkinson, frothed that his session included, 'the best backhand tubes of my life'.

That day showcased Mundaka at its very best. The morning saw smooth lines pouring into the swollen river mouth. As the tide turned, waves slowly started appearing, and by dead low tide, sets of six to eight feet were draining off a waist-high sandbank before rifling off for as far as 300 metres. Despite the presence of the best surfers in the world, the locals still dominated; their ability to protect their wave with both skill and outright hostility should never be underestimated. Two hours after low tide the switch was flicked, and once again smooth swells ran down the bank, now not even breaking.

But everyone knew that the sand was there. And, more importantly, the natural surfing order was restored – one of the world's most powerful, picturesque and perfect waves was back, better than ever. Let's just hope it stays that way.

mundaka facts

location On the northeast coast of Spain, about 100 km from Bilbao.

getting there Fly into Bilbao, or to Biarritz (a two-hour drive north).

the perfect day A pure north winter swell is matched by a light southerly offshore. The pros have left Europe and the brass-monkey weather hasn't kicked in.

best months October through to March, with the winter months (December–February) the coldest and most consistent, and less crowded.

boards While it can hold 10 feet easily, this place is still all about the barrel, so your normal board, a back-up, plus one four inches bigger will do.

essentials For winter you'll need a 4/3 steamer and booties, gloves and a hood.

accommodation Very affordable hotels and apartments.

other waves The beachies of Bakio (nine km away) offer fun in the small stuff, while the premier big-wave right of Mekanoz is nearby.

nihiwatu
sumba island
ben mondy

This break is probably best known as Occy's Left, which – if you haven't worked it out already or you've recently been lobotomised – is named after Mark 'Occy' Occhilupo. Traditionally you have a wave named after you either because you were the first to surf it or because you surfed it so unbelievably well that it looks like you own the joint. In Occy's case it was the latter, when Jack McCoy captured his blazing performance at the wave while filming the cult surf video *The Green Iguana* back in 1995.

For many this display was Occy at his all-time best; surfing in fluoro-green trunks, destroying the super-playful left with a mix of flair, finesse and raw power. Anyone who saw that three-minute segment has always held an overwhelming desire to surf that wave and, while we're dreaming, to surf it just like Occy. After the video came out, the collective naming of the wave was in a sense inevitable.

But the thing is, that wasn't even a particularly good day at Nihiwatu (also, tellingly, known as 'God's Left'). The man who discovered the wave, Claude Graves, an American who had left Bali to find another unknown Utopia, remembers that day as 'being only four feet and fun, but not epic. Three days after Jack and Occy left, it was as good as it gets.'

One can only imagine the effect the video would have had if these two had stayed on. You see, this wave can get very, very good. It can also hold real size. Jack McCoy, an old friend of Graves, had visited here earlier with that ultimate Indonesian explorer Jim Banks. On that trip they surfed it at 10–12 feet plus. The footage, they say, is incredible, but for a variety of reasons it has never seen the light of day.

The wave is still considered a relatively secret spot, due partly to the isolation, poor transport and poverty of Sumba, but more to the efforts of Graves. Over 20 years he has built up a resort there, and he has exercised exclusive rights to the break since 1997. Inevitably there have been differing views on this. Graves claims he has been a responsible custodian for the protection of the locals' health, culture, customs and environment, things that are usually destroyed whenever a prime surfing spot is opened to the masses. Others argue that no one owns a wave and that surfers and surfing, even unchecked, can have a positive effect on the local economy. Either way, Graves runs a top-end resort at the wave, in one of the most stunning, beautiful and untouched parts of Indonesia. You may have to pay for the privilege, but with a maximum of 10 surfers at any one time you can see why the premium is high.

The wave itself sits directly in front of the resort. Indonesian winter swells wrap out of the depths into a wide bay, hit a sculptured coral reef and wind down for some 275 metres into a deep channel. It has the odd barrel section, but is more known for its wide, steep and ultra-whackable walls. It breaks at three feet, is fun and forgiving up to eight, then holds it own in hyperdrive at 10 feet and over. In short, it has something for everybody. Even the non-surfer – 30 per cent of visitors to the resort are honeymooners.

nihiwatu

location Halfway along the southern coast of the Indonesian island of Sumba.

getting there The closest airport is at Tambolak in West Sumba, which has once-a-week flights from Bali.

the perfect day It's six feet and offshore, you've been surfing like Occy, and the 100-kilo marlin you caught this morning is being served up for dinner tonight.

best months It's best through the typical Indonesian winter season of May–September.

boards An Indonesian quiver (a couple of shortboards and a semi-gun) will suffice, although above 10 feet a 7'2" won't go astray.

essentials A booking at the (pretty pricey) Nihiwatu resort.

accommodation It's expensive, but there aren't many places like it in the world.

other waves There are rumours of other world-class secret spots nearby, but generally there's no need to travel far.

one palm point
panaitin island
d.c. green

Surfing One Palm is a game of Russian roulette with fire-coral bullets. It can deliver tube rides beyond the realm of the conceivable, rides to drive an android mad. But everyone who surfs here must pay the price – in blood. Says Gold Coast ripper Damon Harvey: 'One Palm is the shallowest wave in the world that's regularly surfed. At least with Pipeline, you've got a shoulder. Here, every time I came off, I hit coral.'

Yet another Paul King Indonesian discovery, One Palm, on an island off southwest Java, was first revealed to the world in the late 80s Hot Buttered movie, *Surf Nasties*. Teenagers Kye and Joel Fitz(gerald) scored the barrels of their young lives, while dad Terry preferred a safer pursuit: snowboarding Krakatoa's volcanic ash where two Swedes had died the week before.

My first wave at One Palm was a five-footer with a distinctive shoulder. Perfect, I thought. Right from take-off I was locked into the barrel, and progressively getting deeper. After eight seconds, the foam ball mowed me. My helmeted noggin bounced off coral like a crazed pinball. Rolled across the reef, I rose, shaking, in knee-deep water, bleeding from my shoulder, hip, leg, both arms, feet and hands, with coral lumps poking from my helmet like fiery horns. At One Palm there is no back-off section where a cutback (let alone any other sort of turn) can even be contemplated. Some of the barrels reel so square and shallow that it would be easier to ride a dune buggy along the reef inside the pit – provided it's a V8. As Bill, the cook on the charter boat *Nomad*, says: 'The bottom line, if you're coming to surf these waves, is you'd better know what you're getting into, or don't even bother spending the dollars.'

One Palm is named after the solitary tree rising above the dense native jungle that marks the take-off zone. The first section is heavy, offering eight-second-plus barrels. Often there's no escape, and you have to keep riding into the second section, which is even longer and heavier. The third and seemingly endless final section is for the insane, kamikaze and supremely skilled only. Rides of more than 500 metres (and beyond) are possible; I timed one wave of US feral Travis Potter, resplendent in his 3/2 steamer, at over 80 seconds. Forget the ratings. There's no lefthander (let alone a right!) in our solar system that can touch this baby, let alone in Indo.

Too many surferrs will undoubtedly choke this paradise. At least the Mentawai chain has lots of islands. Here, the unpeopled environment is fragile, and the surf spots few and fickle. Sadly, One Palm faces multiple threats: overzealous fishermen; nearby Krakatoa, famous for making the biggest explosion in modern history, in 1883, now smoking and ready to blow again. And, worst of all, developers. In 2005, a controversial land camp was built on the island, closer to a swamp than to any waves. The Friends of Panaitan Island group is still fighting the camp's legality. Creating Kuta Mark II here is especially insane considering that Panaitan was hitherto uninhabited and is part of the Ujung Kulon National Park, one of only two UNESCO World Heritage Areas in Indonesia. It is home to numerous species of rare and endangered plants and animals, including deer, panthers, tigers and the Javan rhinoceros (just 60 left in the world).

one palm point facts

location   Just off the southwestern tip of Java.

getting there   Fly to Indonesia's capital, Jakarta.
A three-hour bemo ride and six-hour boat trip follow.

the perfect day   Giant swell that will wrap in
and become six–eight feet. Mid-tide, and an offshore
trade wind.

best months   April–October (dry season).

boards   Big board to get in early. Small board to
pump and turn in the barrel.

essentials   Skin protection
(booties, helmet, full body armour),
sunscreen, medical kit. Comprehensive
travel and medical insurance (don't
forget your permit!)

accommodation   Land camp
(cough). Numerous charter yachts ply
these waters, including the *Nomad*.

other waves   Apocalypse
(across the bay from One Palm),
Napalms and a newly discovered
mega-bombie: all heavy hitters.

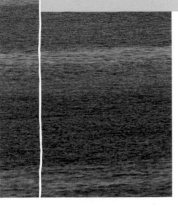

pasta point
maldives
sean doherty

The Maldives are amongst the lowest-lying islands in the world. Of the 1192 sand islands and coral atolls that make up the chain, the highest point is only two metres above sea level. And while above sea level there's not much more than white sand and palm trees, for surfers the islands' real treasures lie beneath the surface, for the Maldives are home to some of the world's most playful surfing reefs.

The story of the discovery of surf in the Maldives is a classic case of serendipity. Back in 1973, Sydney surfers Tony Hinde and Mark Scanlon were sailing their yacht from Sri Lanka across to Africa when they were blown off-course by monsoon winds and ran aground on the shores of Male Atoll in the central Maldives. While waiting for their boat to be salvaged, the pair noticed several reefs with clear surfing potential; in time they realised they'd run aground on a surfing Utopia. Hinde never returned home, and today his surf-travel business is based within a stone's throw from the lefts of Pasta Point.

The islands being so low, the 2004 Boxing Day tsunami wreaked havoc here. Aussie surfer Steve Lanfranco was in the water at the time: 'The first thing we saw was all the bats and birds just rise up into the sky. And the surge lasted for no longer than 10 minutes, and then as quickly as it came it sucked back out again. So it went from the highest tide I've ever seen to the lowest. When we got back to our *dhoni* [the local boat] we were seeing all sorts of stuff floating in the water – big shipping crates, upturned boats, jetties from islands.' But it is the low-lying nature of the islands that gives the waves here their uniquely fun quality. Unlike places such as Tahiti, the Maldives coral reefs drop slowly into deeper water, taking much of the sting out of the swell.

Named in honour of the island resort's original Italian owners, Pasta Point is regarded as the best wave in the region. It's a long, walling left, with a defined barrel section (the Macaroni Bowl) and a racy inside section (Lockjaws). It picks up more swell than anywhere else in the island chain, and is better protected from the wind. It can handle eight feet of swell; during June and July, long-fetch swells from the Roaring 40s consistently march their way north. A full day's surfing here will indeed leave your arms feeling like overcooked linguine. The real beauty of Pasta, though, is the array and proximity of waves within a short *dhoni* ride. Sultans and Honky's wrap around opposite sides of the small island to the south – Honky's the left, Sultans the right. It's like something you'd draw as a kid daydreaming in maths class.

To surf Pasta Point you have to be a guest at Dhonveli Beach and Spa (before you feel an aching sensation in your back pocket, the tariff is a fraction of what you'd pay on an island like Tavarua). While the camp caters for 100 people, the number of surfers is limited to 30, many of whom hail from countries of limited surfing pedigree, like Germany and Kazakhstan. The boats are punctual and the crowds manageable, and you get access to all the waves in the vicinity. Tourism is strictly regulated in the Maldives – you can't just wing it, and need to pre-book your accommodation. But while there are surfboat charters and other resorts, Dhonveli is the one that gives you access to Pasta.

Anyway, you won't have too much time – during the 50-metre walk from your bungalow to the Pasta Point break – to ponder any ethical issues you may have about staying in an exclusive surf resort. And a beer on the deck, watching the sun sink into the firing line-up, will seal the deal.

pasta point facts

location   Kanu Huraa Island, eastern reef of North Male Atoll, Maldives.

getting there   Fly into Male, after which it's a 30-minute speedboat ride across to Dhonveli.

the perfect day   Six feet of southerly to southeast swell, with light northwest to northeast winds. Just you, Hans and Borat in the line-up.

best months   Between April and October (the *Halhangu*, or wet season), although June and July tend to drag in the most swell.

boards   Your normal shortboards will do nicely, plus one bigger board in case you cop a swell and one fish/funboard in case you don't.

essentials   A small bucket of sunscreen, an ability to plan your day's surfing itinerary with military efficiency to avoid the crowds.

accommodation   As noted, Dhonveli Resort if you want to surf Pasta Point, though guests staying at nearby (far more expensive) Four Seasons Resort can also sometimes get day passes.

other waves   There are heaps of them: Cokes, Chickens, Honky's, Lohi's and Sultans, to name just a few in the general vicinity. The Maldives also has incredible waves in its southern atolls, the surf potential of which is only just starting to be tapped.

piha bar
new zealand
derek morrison

Piha is widely considered to be the birthplace of modern surfing in New Zealand. Though various forms of surfing have long been a part of life for coastal Maori groups, it was on these warping left walls that Kiwis were first exposed to modern surfboard design and began to produce their own locally grown boards.

Rick Stoner and Bing Copeland , a couple of Yanks from Los Angeles sailed into Auckland Harbour in November 1958 and found their way out to Piha, where they surfed the waves like they'd never been surfed before. Built by Dale Velzy in California, the Americans' boards had a shaped balsa core covered with fibreglass matting and resin. They were much shorter and lighter than existing boards – so it was much easier to surf across the face of a wave and do turns. Local Peter Byers befriended the two travellers and worked alongside them as they scoured Auckland for materials to build five new boards. After four months, Stoner and Copeland returned to America, and Byers bought and completed the unfinished boards.

Following the rapid proliferation of modern boards Piha, wrongly or rightly, became etched in history as one of the hotbeds of New Zealand surfing. Today it still flies its 'New Zealand's Most Famous Surf Beach' flag in a faintly optimistic figure-of-eight motion.

On its day, Piha certainly deserves lofty accolades. White water soars 10 metres into the air off the back of Camel Rock to signal a set grinding its way around the corner of the stony mass. The arriving peak shuffles left and right before lurching into a wedge at take-off, then reeling towards Lion Rock with random bowl sections looming according to the sand deposits en route. The relatively short 50–80-metre wall terminates in a very sucky end section that has a reputation for snapping boards and bodies. Piha can handle very clean swells up to eight feet, but hits its optimum around the six-foot range. The bigger it gets, and the lower the tide, the faster the circulation of the currents and rips. From four feet on, it quickly becomes a treacherous place for the inexperienced, with shallow sandbars sucking you back into the impact zone like a giant magnet, and currents across the bars making your escape an oxygen-sapping struggle.

Surfing Piha is an adventure which even begins when you're paddling out. The easy option is in the rip that hugs the rocky shoreline of Camel Rock. The current sweeps out from the lagoon past Patiki Rock, and all you have to do is time your dash through the line-up to the back of the bar. Too early and you'll be swept into the vortex of an end section and wash up back on the beach; too late and you'll risk wearing a set on the head with a lip so thick it'll feel like you've just insulted Jake 'the Muss' at the peak of one of his reages in *Once Were Warriors*. But the real adventure lies a little further south, on the far rim of the lagoon, where a natural crack in Camel Rock forms the Keyhole. This is the appropriate point of initiation for the brave. It's a 30-metre, narrow cave that exits the rocky outcrop just inside the peak of Piha Bar, the entry being its emptying point into the lagoon. It can only be navigated at mid–low tide, when it's big, and will often require 10 or more duck-dives (in darkness) to get to the cave's mouth. Crabs scurry around the walls as you're forced to time your final exit with the utmost aplomb or risk being washed back into the cave – or, worse, smeared across the rocks. If your natural timing is good then this will deliver you into the line-up with surprising ease. If not, you will join the throngs of surfers who tell of being pinned against the roof as the cave filled with water, being stranded on a ledge at the cave's mouth and duck-diving walls of white water inside the cave itself.

Piha can be many things, but it's always a journey.

piha bar facts

location   Around 50 km northwest of Auckland, on the central west coast of New Zealand's North Island.

getting there   Fly into Auckland, which is a scenic 40-minute drive away.

the perfect day   Six feet of groomed southwest swell from a deep Tasman Sea low. A light offshore southeast wind to iron out the last few kinks.

best months   October–June produces the best conditions for Piha. Mid-winter swells (July–August) are often accompanied by ferocious and persistent southwest and westerly airstreams that turn west-coast beaches into giant, frothy washing machines.

boards   If it's five feet plus, you'll need something an inch or two longer than your normal beachie board just to help you get into the waves early and paddle out of the vortexes on the end section. If it's less than five feet, anything from 6'2" to 6'6" will work. Drivey tails, bottoms and fins will help you make warping sections.

essentials   Boardies in the peak of summer, a springy through late spring to early autumn, and expect to pull out a 4/3 steamer in winter. There is no fuel at Piha, so fill up on the way in. The New Zealand sun burns intensely, even on cloudy days, so cover up.

accommodation   Various options, including cabins, camping and a backpackers.

other waves   North Piha has consistent banks with a left and right peak off the north side of Lion Rock. Caves is sheltered from a northeast wind and provides some quality rights. Karekare, to the south of Piha, offers some respite from the crowds and its shallow sandbanks often produce barrels.

pipeline
hawaii
sean doherty

In Hawaiian culture, where surfing is the measure of a man, Pipeline is the measure of a surfer. For the guys whose lives revolve around surfing Pipe, the experience is as much spiritual as it is routine, and there's a ritual element to the act of just paddling out. To be considered a true legend of the sport, you need to have some sort of pedigree out here; Lopez, Carroll, Slater and Irons have all shot to glory from the gaping green caverns of this place.

After years of hearing the stories, watching the movies and staring at the photos, you drive along the Kam Highway expecting Pipeline to be guarded by a bronzed statue of Gerry Lopez next to a flashing billboard with the names of the Pipe Masters winners in the carpark. On a small day, however, you could walk right past it and not even know it was there. A nondescript peak on a stretch of beach that looks pretty much like any other. Add 12 feet of pure west swell, however, and suddenly a liquid Godzilla rises from the ocean. To sit on the beach and watch Pipeline in full cry is one thing – to surf it is another.

The reef at Pipe is actually three reefs staggered one behind the other, heading out to sea. Third Reef Pipe is the big daddy, breaking 200 metres out and only rearing its head when the swell is enormous. Third Reef refracts the lines of swell and helps create the famous Pipeline A-frame on the two inside reefs. Second Reef Pipe is a big, old hydraulic peak that starts breaking at eight feet and goes up from there. This is when Pipe is at its best, as the Second Reef peak is forgiving enough to let you paddle in and sweetly set up the infamous First Reef barrel.

The Pipeline of surfing legend is First Reef. Breaking just 50 metres from shore, the rifling lefthand pit is unpredictable, deathly shallow – and downright glorious. For the purposes of this piece, we'll include Backdoor, the righthander on the other side of the Pipeline peak. After all, if you've travelled 10 000 kilometres to surf Pipeline, we're sure the extra 10 metres to surf Backdoor isn't too much of a stretch. While Pipe breaks around the contour of the reef and into deeper water, Backdoor breaks across a chest-deep shelf and consequently is abrupt and even more dangerous than its next-door neighbour. While it doesn't handle the same swell as Pipe, it's undoubtedly the better barrel of the two.

To properly appreciate the sketchiness of the place, don a mask and flippers on a flat day and inspect the ocean floor here. The fossilised limestone reef isn't a flat platform, but, rather, a series of craggy caves and pinnacles that look like a twisted moonscape. You can fathom why this place has claimed more lives than any other wave on Earth. The last fatality there was on 3 December 2005, when Tahitian surfer Malik Joyeux took off an eight-foot set, hit the bottom, and never came up. His death rocked the Pipeline surf community, and the really scary thing here is that Malik was regarded as one of the world's most talented big-wave surfers. Surfing it is an exercise in respect, even for the best guys.

To sit on the beach and watch Pipeline in full cry is one thing – to surf it is another.

You don't see too many stand-up comedians in Hawaii and, as if the wave wasn't enough, the human element at Pipe is often more dangerous than the wave itself. Pipeline

is the most contested, ruthless and regulated line-up in the world. Only breaking for five months a year, you can count on one hand the classic days each season. In November and December, when the pro tour is in town, the place is a complete basket-case, and the only semblance of order comes from the enforcing presence of the local 'Wolfpak'.

The world's population is divided into three categories: those who haven't surfed Pipe, those who've paddled out when it's three feet and claim they've surfed it, and those who have actually surfed it when it's *real* Pipe. The best way to find yourself in this last category is to make your North Shore pilgrimage post-Christmas. The pro-tour circus has left town, the local guys have chilled out, and the chickens and dogs have taken back the streets. This is when you'll see the real North Shore and, hopefully, the real Pipeline.

pipeline 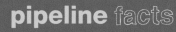facts

location   North Shore of Oahu Island, Hawaii.

getting there   Fly into Honolulu, from where it's a one-hour drive to North Shore.

the perfect day   Eight–10 foot of clean west swell, enough for Second Reef to fire; no sand on First Reef. A mid-morning paddle out to avoid the morning wobble.

best months   Pipe breaks between October and March, but October to December are chaotic, to say the least. January through to March will still be crowded, but will give you a better shot at snaring your trophy wave.

boards   You'll need to start somewhere around the 6'3" mark for the smallest days, then work your way up to 7'0"–7'4" when Second and Third Reefs start showing.

essentials   A really good set of boards, a willingness to surf harder than you've ever surfed before.

accommodation   If you're cashed up, you can rent a house along the Sunset Beach to Log Cabins stretch. There is some more modest backpacker accommodation down toward Waimea Bay. Or you can always stay in cheaper digs in Honolulu and drive out.

other waves   You're on the North Shore for chrissake, there are plenty! Off the Wall is 50 m away, Rocky Point 500 m away, Sunset Beach around 1.5 km away.

p-pass
caroline islands
kirk owers

Beau Emerton says this is the best wave he's ever surfed. Brendan Margieson reckons he's never had so many tubes on a surf trip. Dylan Longbottom describes it as 'by far the best righthander in the world'.

You'll find these and other glowing tributes by some of the world's most widely travelled surfers recorded in the guestbook at Pohnpei Surf Club. The wave in question, a powerful tubing reef break known as P-Pass (Palikir Pass), has put the sleepy Caroline Islands well and truly on the map.

The 500 islands, reefs and atolls which make up the Carolines are scattered across the Pacific Ocean north of New Guinea and east of the Philippines. Isolation, transport hassles and expense have kept surf travel in the area to bare bones until recent years. In October 2004 the Caroline's first surf camp opened its doors and interest in the area sky rocketed almost immediately. Saturation coverage and mouth-watering images in the world's premier surf magazines have painted it as one of this century's most exciting surf discoveries.

National Geographic, strangely, was the publication that started the ball rolling. In 1987 a Brazilian surfer, Allois Malfitani, was flicking through its pages when he came across a photo of an enticing, empty reef pass. Later, when he was living in Hawaii (and running Mark Foo's infamous North Shore backpacker lodge), he encountered the magazine again and made plans to find the wave. It led Allois to Micronesia and, eventually, to Palikir Pass. Today Allois is joint owner and surf guide at Pohnpei Surf Club and is happy to share the story of his first surf at P-Pass: 'There was not a single soul for as far as the eye could see. Outside the breakers a big school of fish and hundreds of birds diving for baitfish . . . then suddenly a set came by and peeled perfectly along the reef. For the first time ever I put on a helmet and could hear my heart beating inside it. I caught one, two, three waves until I got one that really walled up. When it slingshot me through the bowl I knew I had found something special.'

For years Allois surfed in seclusion, or with friends he'd convinced to return with him to the Carolines. Eventually he decided a surf camp was inevitable. Why not do it himself? Today one of the best things about surfing P-Pass and the surrounding breaks is that crowds are minimal. The Pohnpei Surf Club handles a maximum of 17 surfers at any one time and there are no plans to increase numbers. There are good set-ups on the east and west sides of the islands but the best breaks, such as P-Pass, are found on the northwest coast. P-Pass is great fun at two feet, a good barrel up to five feet and a serious, experts-only drainpipe at six–eight feet. On big days it can be compared to a reverse Teahupoo; the wave bends around the reef and is fast and thick, wipe-outs are memorable, and barrels are intense.

Micronesia is not ideally placed to receive huge amounts of swell. As is the

On big days it can be compared to a reverse Teahupoo; the wave bends around the reef and is fast and thick, wipe-outs are memorable, and barrels are intense.

case with the Philippines it relies on North Pacific lows which track eastwards towards Hawaii and offer short windows of swell. During the island's seven-month swell season P-Pass typically gets 10 days of four–six-foot swell a month, with the occasional bigger day. While it doesn't adhere too readily to set patterns, when the swell hits it's generally pumping.

Gary 'Kong' Elkerton is a regular visitor and raves about the place at any given opportunity. His entry in the Pohnpei Surf Club guestbook enthusiastically sums up the Caroline Island experience: 'Been around the world a million times. Seen the best waves in the world, but this trip was one of the best. P-Pass is sick at two feet and at eight to 10 the place is unbelievable.'

p-pass facts

location   Caroline Islands, north of Papua New Guinea and the Solomons, in Micronesia, South Pacific.

getting there   Book with worldsurfaris.com or fly to Pohnpei and start searching.

the perfect day   Six-foot north swell. Mirror glass. You and five of your best mates. Every wave a barrel, and every barrel a little deeper than the last.

best months   The season runs from October to April. Allois Malfitani says the best swell month changes every year.

boards   If you score swell you'll need some length. Add a few inches to your shortboard regardless, as this is a powerful wave. Two boards minimum.

essentials   Plenty of sunscreen, and a good medical kit for reef cuts.

accommodation   Pohnpei Surf Club (PSC) offer airconditioned bungalows, dedicated charter boats and experienced guides.

other waves   There are half a dozen other quality waves nearby. The Carolines' myriad islands and atolls are mostly untouched by surfers.

puerto escondido
mexico
dave sparkes

Puerto has established itself as a truly iconic wave, a thundering beach-break barrel that inspires awe and respect from surfers worldwide. It is one of the few waves to be given the honourable title of 'Pipeline', which says more about its aura than anything else

While the break is commonly known as Puerto Escondido, this is actually the name of the town that hosts the beach, which itself is called Zicatela. Puerto Escondido means 'hidden port', and the place earned this title back in the days when access was extremely difficult. Though the area was inhabited for centuries by the indigenous Indians, the town itself was established in 1928 as a coffee export port. When Highway 200 opened up the region and radically improved access in the late 1960s, western travellers started catching on.

A couple of Texan surfers had discovered the wave in around 1959, but it wasn't until the early 70s that the penny really dropped. The first magazine cover and story, featuring giant tubes and an air of delicious mystery, let the cat out of the bag, and the addition of a major airport has seen development run wild, with tourists and surfers arriving in droves. The nightlife is becoming legendary and a classic circuit has evolved, taking you right through until dawn via a series of increasingly rowdy options beginning with dinner and ending with crazed dancing at sunrise.

The first magazine cover and accompanying story featuring giant tubes and an air of delicious mystery, let the cat out of the bag.

Zicatela Beach is right across the road from the town's bars, hotels and shops, making access as easy as stumbling across the street and jumping in. The northern end of the beach features a fast, hollow right bank known as Carmelita's, which breaks in very shallow water and is heavily surfed, becoming quite crowded at times. The real deal, however, is the Far Bar, a massive left further down the beach which holds up to 20 feet and breaks more boards than any other wave on Earth (this has resulted in a fast-growing business for local entrepreneurs, who can have your board ready to be broken again by next morning). The waves here have a reputation for tending to close out, but it all depends on who you talk to. For most, the chance of being spat out of a 15–20-foot beach-break tube is worth a few false leads into oblivion. Zicatela is an early riser's heaven, as the onshore south wind hits at around 11 a.m. every day

Local surfers have really established themselves here and very much run the show; mess with them and you'll be given your marching orders quick smart. Celestino and Omar Diaz, Carlos Nogales, Roberto Salinas, Oscar Moncada and a few others are the movers and shakers, and generally get all the best waves – and that's the way it should be.

puerto escondido facts

location   On the south coast of Mexico, about 240 km south of Oaxaca City.

getting there   Fly to Mexico City, then catch a domestic flight to Puerto Escondido. The hardcore route is to fly to Oaxaca City and then drive to Puerto.

the perfect day   10-foot straight south swell, light north winds.

best months   July–September (rainy season).

boards   Everything you have, plus something bigger. Smaller days can be fun, but you really need at least a 7'6" or even an 8'0" – we're talking huge, Hawaiian-style pits here. Get the boards heavily glassed to at least delay their demise a bit.

essentials   Sunblock, tube nous, readiness to party at night, and even more guns.

accommodation   There are a million options, from cheap to expensive depending on your budget and inclination, but you definitely won't have to be far from the beach.

other waves   La Punta, at the eastern end of the beach, is a fun and workable left point that offers great respite from the intensity of Zicatela. Further south are many other fine waves: a local guide is the way to go.

raglan
new zealand
kirk owers

New Zealand has thousands of quality surf breaks, but only Raglan is truly world-renowned. Its long cool lefts have been on the radar of travelling surfers since their legendary appearance in *Endless Summer* (1964). Raglan is a haven for surfers of all abilities, serving up epic, high-performance leg-burners when conditions align. Its position mid-way down the North Island's west coast ensures consistent swells in a country known for its fickle surf.

Raglan, named after a British baron, was originally known as Whaingaroa, 'the long pursuit'. According to Maori legend a migratory canoe tracked down the west coast using Karioi, the mountain which overlooks Raglan, as a guide. On arrival they discovered the bar was impassable and were forced further south (presumably the surf was cranking). Certainly, after a 500-metre ride at the break known as Indicators ('Indies'), the return paddle can seem an exceedingly long pursuit.

Raglan today is a groovy little tourist town which draws surfers from around the globe. There's one pub, one surf shop, a few cafes and a selection of cheapish accommodation. It may be New Zealand's most famous surf town – and locals may complain it's overrun – but it still has a laid-back country vibe. Maori culture remains strong in the region and its true locals deserve respect. One such man, Richie Rima, was labelled the Mayor of Raglan in a *Tracks* article; if you see a dark-skinned Iggy Pop surfing in undies, say hello to Richie. Rima's small stature and wiry frame belie his legendary ability in a scuffle.

The first thing you notice about the waves at Raglan is that there's a bunch of them. Like a cool-water G-land, Raglan is an umbrella title given to a collection of adjoining lefthand points. There are three main breaks, which are each divisible into two distinct parts that have their advantages depending on your skill level and comfort in a crowd. All are nice and long, and offer plenty of wall – they don't call New Zealand 'the Land of the Long White Lefts' for nothing. Closest to town, Manu Bay picks a little less swell but has the fastest, roundest sections. It breaks on boulders, and features a steep, jacking take-off before running into an even shallower wave known as the Ledge. This is where you're most likely to get barrelled, but it's also the zone favoured by the local rulers. Manu Bay, sometimes called simply 'the Point', is the first wave you come across and usually the most crowded.

Beyond Manu is Whale Bay, also known as the Valley. A large, annoyingly located rock divides this wave in half unless the swell is big and the tide low. It's the slowest-moving wave and is favoured by intermediates, cruisers and longboards. Further out again is Indicators and, beyond that, Outside Indicators. These stately points pick up the most swell and offer fast, super-long rides with plenty of steep walls and the occasional barrel section. It's a fair hike out, which keeps the crowds down.

While Raglan works in small swells, an offshore-brushed, six–eight-foot long fetch is something to behold. Stacked lines peel perfectly down the six points for a distance of three kilometres. You can start at Outside Indicators and surf your way down the strip, picking off several 400-metres-plus rides. Waves of over a kilometre are not unheard-of on the rare days when several of the waves link up. Viewed from a distance and compressed through a telescopic lens, the whole set-up – line after elongated line – makes for one of the most classic line-up photos you can imagine.

raglan facts

location About 40 km northwest of Hamilton, on the west coast of New Zealand's North Island.

getting there Fly to Auckland, a two-hour drive north, or directly to Hamilton (a 30-minute drive).

the perfect day Six-foot low tide at Manu Bay. Take off at Boneyards, race down the line and backdoor the Ledge.

best months Consistent swell year-round, biggest and coldest between May and September. Autumn (March–May) is a good option.

boards Your standard high-performance shortboard, with channels for extra speed, and a fish hybrid for the small days.

essentials A 3/2 steamer will suffice until May; winter requires a 4/3. Booties are a good idea if you're unfamiliar with boulder scrambling.

accommodation The best digs are outside town, overlooking the waves.

other waves New Zealand has more than 15 000 km of surfable coastline. Nearby Ruapuke Beach picks up swell when Raglan is tiny.

restaurants
fiji
sean doherty

If the surfing dream in the 70s was to hike through the malaria-riddled Indonesian jungle to find your own wave and your own personal Buddha, then a week at Restaurants is the surfing dream of the present decade. Wrapping around the back corner of Tavarua Island Resort, Restaurants has been described as the most perfect lefthander in the world, with the perfection existing on both sides of the high-tide line. When your body's vulcanised and your brain fried from a day of insane surf, you can kick back on the deck of the restaurant that gave the wave its name, and quaff cocktails while watching the sun sink into the line-up. In a surfing society that increasingly craves convenience, Restaurants is the ultimate in five-star pay-to-play.

On an island skirted by world-class waves, Restaurants is the jewel. The heart-shaped island faces smack into the Tasman Sea swell window, and it's the island itself that bends the prevailing southwesterly swell 90°, wrapping it around into the leeward side of the island. From the ledging take-off boil, the wave is basically a flawless, 200-metre, breathing, hissing wormhole that gives you no other option than to pull in and race the thing to the death.

To contemplate turns out here is to contemplate life without skin. Unlike its neighbour, Cloudbreak, Restaurants isn't open to the brunt of day-to-day swell, and as a result the reef here is teeming with coral in a million shapes and shades. Some look like giant orange mushrooms, others like the skewery fingers of Satan. The one thing all these corals have in common, though, is the propensity to flay you alive, and any contact with the reef here will draw blood. Be warned – stay away from the bottom half of the tide.

Restaurants is the proverbial goofy's paradise, and surfing the place on your backhand has two distinct disadvantages. First up, while those goofies can just park it and cruise on their forehand, you'll need to have a pretty handy pigdog to make it out of these things. Second, and most disconcertingly, as you shoot along on your backhand you are looking directly down at the reef all the way. If you do end up with a set of tiger claws across your back, medical assistance is at your disposal – which generally involves one of the local girls squeezing a lime into your cuts (they'll hear you scream several kilometres away, in the line-up at Cloudbreak).

As the island sits inside the fringing reef, it takes quite a bit of swell for Restaurants to get going. If Cloudbreak is six feet, as a general rule Restaurants will just be showing at two–three feet. For Restaurants to max out at six to eight feet, Cloudbreak will be 12 to 15. During the southern-hemisphere winter the swell is consistent, so you'd be unlucky during this time to miss surfing Restaurants at least once. As far as winds go, you don't want too much, as the local trade-wind blows cross-shore into the end section as it wraps around the island.

In terms of crowds, it's just going to be you and whoever else can afford the hefty tariff. There are plenty of people willing to pay it, as the island is booked up almost three years in advance. For the price you get exclusive access not only to Restaurants but to Cloudbreak and Tavvy Rights as well, and all the boat transfers, fishing, snorkelling, seafood buffets, Fijian hospitality and banana daiquiris you could possibly want. And if you can't afford it, then there's sure to be an undiscovered, malaria-infested, third-world point break out there somewhere, just waiting for you to trek through the jungle for three weeks to find it – and we're sure you'll get out of it a bit cheaper.

restaurants facts

location   Tavarua Island in the Mamanuca island chain, Fiji.

getting there   Fly to Nadi, where you'll be shuttled by bus and then Fijian longboat out to Tavarua.

the perfect day   Four to five feet of clean southwest swell, light trade winds.

best months   April–September.

boards   Your standard shortboards will do the trick nicely for Restaurants. You don't want too big a board, as you'll be required to do some nimble tube-weaving.

essentials   Several credit cards, plenty of sunscreen, booties if you want to save your feet. And a willingness to surf day and night to get your money's worth.

accommodation   The bures of the resort.

other waves   The bad news is that you've only really got two options. The good news is that both of these options are world-class — both Cloudbreak and Tavvy Rights often produce barrels.

rincon
usa
sean doherty

Just as hundreds of Muslims are trampled to death every year while making their annual pilgrimage to Mecca, travelling to Rincon may result in a similar fate. With California possessing the same surfing population as the entire continent of Australia, and Freeway 101 running alongside it, it's little wonder that the US west coast's best wave often gets a little busy.

On any given day, the cobblestone point at Rincon is a microcosm of Californian surfing. The line-up is a mix of hard-ass locals, pontificating longboarders, rabid grommets, and every sub-species of surfer in between.

The generally friendly nature of the wave here means it can be ridden by pretty well anyone, which results in the line-up often being clogged by human flotsam. The creek mouth that divides the wave also marks the boundary between Santa Barbara and Ventura counties, so there are more claims on the waves here than on the estate of J. Howard Marshall. One thing's for sure – there's nothing boring about a session out at Rincon.

Kevin Costner might live on the point at Rincon, but it doesn't guarantee him a wave out there. Nor does he qualify as Rincon's favourite son – that title will be held for the best part of eternity by Tom Curren. Growing up in neighbouring Santa Barbara, the three-time world champion was weaned on Rincon's long righthand walls, and they chiselled the edges off what was to become the smoothest style of any surfer to dig toes into wax. Lopez and Pipe, Peterson and Kirra – there have been fewer more intimate relationships between man and wave than Curren and Rincon. Jamie Brisick recalls seeing this synergy in a 16-year-old prodigy. 'Curren appeared on the scene in the late afternoon, a flash of speed and style across the head-high, backlit Rincon walls. He was mesmerising, prodigious, artful – there was an incredible oneness between Curren and Rincon, not just when he was up and riding, but in the whole holistic dance. The way he paddled, the way he negotiated the current, positioned himself in the line-up . . . it was all so harmonious.'

They call Rincon 'the Queen of the Coast', and with good reason. While there are two other classic waves that share its name (at Bells Beach and in Puerto Rico, Rincon meaning 'corner' in Spanish), it's the Californian wave that's the real gem. It's a bit like Goldie Locks and the Three Bears: Indicators, the outside point, is a little slow; the middle section – Rivermouth – can be a little fast; on the inside the Cove, however, is just right. If you connected all three sections you'd ride for almost 1.5 kilometres, and you'd be very lucky. Rincon, depending on the swell, tends to section, and if that doesn't halt your golden run, a longboarder no doubt will.

The other reason for the rabid line-up is the fact that Rincon has a narrow swell window and doesn't break classically all that often. Sitting in the swell shadow of the Channel Islands, Rincon won't pick up south swell, and relies entirely on North Pacific winter swells from the north and west to light up. The parabolic shape of the point means it can handle some real swell – 10 feet at least – and these rare bomb swells tend to sort the pretenders from the contenders. But while the creek that runs out halfway down the point gives the break a steady supply of sand, and its trademark browny-yellow backlit tinge, it also flushes a lot of crap from nearby suburbia.

Why would you travel halfway around the world to surf Rincon? One good wave would be sufficient to answer that question, but you don't come here just to surf. You come to sample the giddy human circus that is southern and central California – and you get plenty of chance to do that in the line-up at Rincon.

rincon facts

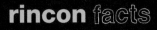

location   Just off Freeway 101, about 24 km south of Santa Barbara, California.

getting there   Fly to Los Angeles, then hire a car for the drive up the coast (around 110 km).

the perfect day   Eight feet of west swell, light northwest winds.

best months   September–March, as the place needs big North Pacific swells to come to life.

boards   Your normal shortboard will do the trick. However, in the interests of blending in with the crowd you might want to ride a longboard.

essentials   A willingness to deal with large numbers of human beings.

accommodation   Plenty in nearby Carpinteria or Santa Barbara.

other waves   There's plenty of good surf in the area, including the Ranch, Sandspit and Hammonds. But access (and, in the case of Sandspit, water quality) are problems.

st clair
new zealand
derek morrison

If any city is to claim the mantle as New Zealand's premier surf city then it has to be Dunedin. Its urban sprawl shuffles the four kilometres from the city centre to the coast like a king tide. Its open ocean frontage takes in three point breaks, numerous permanent sandbars and five kilometres of white sandy beach littered with dark-blue peaks.

Though hardly the best wave in the area, St Clair Point has become the focus of city surfers. The righthand point (and sneaky left) can be fat, wobbly and inhospitable at times, but have mastered the knack of cleaning up before the cinnamon dusting has settled on your cappuccino from the fishbowl coffee shop overlooking the break.

The south coast of the South Island is the most wave-rich coastline in New Zealand. Southwest and southerly swells generated by the relentless Roaring 40s are channelled between Stewart Island and the mainland. Hasty grooming takes place when they're forced to wrap northward along the Catlins coastline before unloading, just over 200 kilometres away, on Otago's south coast.

It's at St Clair Point that most first-time Dunedin surfers try out, and for most it's worse than expected. Southern Ocean currents flow coolly along the coastline, restricting average winter temperatures to 9°C, with a stifling 14°C average in summer. Dunedin, it is said, is one of the few places where you have to duck-dive icebergs – in the winter of 2006 that proved to be more than a myth, when several massive Antarctic ice-bergs drifted to within 90 kilometres of the coast. On rare occasions, there's even a light dusting of snow on the beaches. But St Clair can deliver enough quality to help you forget you're not wearing boardies. At six feet, the wave begins with an ominous line that wanders in from the south searching for a place to come to rest. It begins to stumble awkwardly on the submerged rock ledges that precede the take-off zone, before lurching left, standing up tall and buckling into a feathery peak.

On the right tide, water drains off the kelp-forested rocky ledges, fronds jack-knife out of the water, and kelp heads burst through the surface like angry sea creatures. The peak collapses to the left in a violent explosion (on smaller swells, a very punchy left can be had by the opportunistic) and the right begins to peel at a hurried pace, though the face itself is more of a fun, carving wall. This section runs for 20–30 metres before the wave changes shape and hits the second ledge. This is the take-off zone on smaller days, but on big days it's a fast, bowly section that often opens up into a wild pit. If the swell pushes too wide on the point, the wave fattens out from here on in with an unremarkable end section that is just promising enough to entice you along but is mostly fruitless. If the swell kinks after the bowl (which it often does in smaller conditions) you can pick up the racy inside that skirts the edge of the submerged kelp forest.

The University of Otago offers the perfect cover for surfers looking for an extended three–five-year holiday. The students also add character to the city, bringing a vibrant nightlife and an infectious laid-back approach – fuelled, of course, by the local Speights brew. Dunedin surfing is a rich experience in the raw-ness both of the Southern Ocean and of its inhabitants. Every year that the New Zealand national surfing championship has visited here, at least one top-seed has been chased out of contention by St Clair's resident leopard seal or an equally dis-gruntled fur seal. It's always the out-of-towners who get picked on by the seals, and it's all carried out in such a theatrical manner that you'd almost think someone has put them up to it. Then again, this is Dunedin, so that may just be the case . . .

st clair facts

location On the southeast coast of New Zealand's South Island, five minutes southeast of Dunedin.

getting there Dunedin's international airport (formerly a prize dairy farm) is just 20 minutes drive from the city. The other option is to fly into Christchurch and drive the four hours to Dunedin from there.

the perfect day Eight feet of direct south swell, a mild northwest breeze to help it stand up, and a middle to low tide.

best months April through to November sees the most southern swell activity, though you will have to pick your times — it will range from scary to eye-watering perfection during each weather cycle through winter.

boards You could surf most swells at St Clair Point on a good beachie board, though extra length and volume will aid paddling on windy days and help you make freight-train sections. A bigger board is strongly recommended if you intend to sample some of the other waves in the area.

essentials Pack a 2/3 or 3/4 steamer for summer; invest in a 3/4 (or 3/4/5) steamer, booties, hood, gloves and insulated rash vest for winter (or go the whole hog and get a Rip Curl H-Bomb heated wetsuits). You definitely need a car to explore the Otago coastline.

accommodation This is a university city, so accommodation is as plentiful as the pubs and bars. Check out www.cityofdunedin.com as your starting point.

other waves The Otago Peninsula to the north is a treasure just waiting to be explored. The coast south of St Clair is loaded with hidden gems, and any hint of swell from the north turns on the entire north coast like the flick of a switch.

st leu
reunion island
craig jarvis

Due to some horrible glitch, some historical mess-up, bodyboarders have rights at St Leu. It's an amazing thing to see bodyboarders calling surfers off perfect waves, and the surfers obeying.

That aside, this is one very special break. Who can forget a young Occy, hair all done up in plaits, ripping up the inside bowl in one of those old McCoy Billabong videos? *Pump*, I think it was, or *Filthy Habits*. Also home to a number of Association of Surfing Professionals events, from the Yop Reunion Pro to the most recent Rip Curl Pro Search, St Leu is a user-friendly and rippable wave that also throws the occasional thick barrel.

Reunion Island is an offshore French 'department', and its culture is a rich mix of European, African, Indian and Chinese traditions. Add to this a year-round summer and tropical water, as well as a plethora of other waves in the vicinity, and you will understand why St Leu is a paradise for the surfer.

There are just a few things to detract from its perfection. First, it gets hot in summer. Really, really hot. If you're not on the beach cooling off you need to have some airconditioning or be sitting next to a fan with an ice-cold beer in your hand. Second, it does get super-crowded. The good news is that there are plenty of waves here, though you'll have to go a bit further if you're not one for hustling amongst madding crowds.

170

And finally St Leu is pretty expensive. You can, of course, live cheaply, but you need to be really circumspect in order to do so. Your options are limited to the French economy.

St Leu is the wave that you travel to Reunion Island for. Although, as mentioned, there are many other fine waves around, they pale somewhat into insignificance next to St Leu. It's a lined-up coral reef that bends down the line with a number of weird little quirks and habits. The wave has two main sections, the inside being the one that barrels properly. To achieve this, the swell needs to have some west in it, and the swell can't be too big. If swells are bigger than six feet, the wave tends to push through to deeper water and miss the inside section altogether. Swells with no west tend to do the same, just running into deep water outside the inside reef. But when a four–six-foot west swell comes through on the tide and has gone past mid-tide on the way up, there are going to be some tunnels!

The wind does funny things as well. The best wind is the southeaster, but due to the reef wrapping so much it too does strange things. At the top of the point, right by the take-off spot, the wave appears as a ragged, windblown mess. You need to find a line between the cross-chops and get into the wave. It's best to start weaving down the line, staying ahead of the white water, just keeping going. As the wave starts to feel the bend in the reef and wrap accordingly, so the southeast wind becomes more offshore.

> **There are many other fine waves around, but they pale into insignificance next to St Leu. It's a lined-up coral reef that bends down the line with a number of weird little quirks.**

By the time you get to the inside bowl, the wind is directly offshore and the wave will no doubt be just about to barrel over your lucky head. Otherwise, you can sit on the inside and pick off the waves that are already offshore. Chances are there will be someone on them already, however – might even be a bodyboarder.

st leu facts

location   West coast of Reunion Island, about 200 km southwest of Mauritius, in the southern Indian Ocean.

getting there   Fly into the island capital of St Denis. From there it's a taxi ride or a hire car down to St Leu.

the perfect day   Mid-tide pushing, four–six feet, west swell and southeast wind. A weekday, not too many people around.

best months   May–August, although it gets pretty good at any odd time of the year. Less swell in summer, but sublime clean swells come through after the swell season.

boards   If you're only going to surf St Leu, a small board and maybe a medium board/semi-gun. If you're going to explore the island, then you need some bigger boards.

essentials   Bring all your own equipment, as the surf shops are unbelievably expensive. Unless you're loaded, that is, or you earn francs.

accommodation   Lots of options, from campsites to backpackers to self-catering. A nice hotel in the area is the Paladien Apolonia, and there is a reasonably priced VVF (French Government Tourist Office accommodation) as well.

other waves   There are loads of them, but the best two, right there at St Leu, are Turtle Farms and Etang Sale ('dirty pond'). Others worth checking out are Boucan Canot, L'Hermitage reef pass, and fun waves on a small swell, Trois Bassins.

shipstern bluff
australia
sean doherty

Once known as 'Devil's Point', Shipstern Bluff's ferocity seen at close quarters will leave little doubt that this hellish righthander could indeed be a crossover point to the Underworld. For decades this wave was more myth than reality, as no one had even considered surfing it. While its sheer brutality kept surfers out of the water, its splendid isolation at the bottom of Tasmania ensured it stayed off the surfing map. Its latterday pioneering has been one of the great stories of modern surfing, though Shipstern is still regarded as a relatively secret spot (as the vandalised sign at the top of the track will attest to).

Cold, uninhabited, and lashed by the Roaring 40s, the Gold Coast this ain't. Named after the headland that towers over the wave like a fossilised *Titanic*, Shipstern Bluff is as raw a surfing experience as you could wish for. Two-hundred-metre cliffs rise vertically out of the ocean, and if you are looking for a reassuring hint of civilisation you won't find it. The only way in and out of here is either by boat or on foot, and the isolation of the place gives it a sinister vibe – not helped by the fact that the waters here are patrolled by some of the biggest white sharks you could ever hope to avoid.

But in a world where all the best waves are being wantonly developed to the back teeth, to see a wave still as beautiful as it was millennia ago is a breath of fresh air. The wave is so heavy, and the walk in such a pain, that it doesn't attract big crowds, as a result of which the local guys are still pretty mellow. They figure that more surfers in the water lowers their chances of getting chomped.

Rumours of a wave in Tasmania far gnarlier than anything on the main land first drifted across Bass Strait in 2000. Up until that point the true, awful potential of Shipstern Bluff was known only by the local guys who'd already surfed it (at that stage about three of them). Back in 1997, Tasmanian surfer Andy Campbell, who would become synonymous with the wave in coming years, became the first to surf the place. 'Sitting on my surfboard, alone, my legs felt weak from apprehension and fear as they dangled in the cold water. Could anyone ride the infamous Tasmanian wave? Was I the first to try? From that day my surfing took a radical new direction. I had purpose, direction, and my arena was right in my backyard. Pioneering one of the world's heaviest waves has so far been an unforgettable journey that is still far from over.'

On a big swell with a low tide, and full sunlight for dramatic effect, the wave can look like a living Dali painting as it warps, twists and devours itself.

In late 2000 the first visiting mainlanders surfed Shipstern, and the following year pro surfers Kieren Perrow, Mark Mathews and Drew Courtney scored the place at a frightening 10–12 feet while on a *Tracks* magazine photo trip with Tasmanian photographer, Sean Davey. And while the wave's location was never divulged, the images of that day were flashed around the world and the surf media came down with a feverish case of Tasmania. 'Our local guide didn't exactly inspire confidence,' recalls Perrow. 'He looks at the line-up and goes, "You guys shouldn't be going out. I don't

think it's surfable."' Halfway through the session, KP was wishing he'd listened. 'I remember being stuck in a frothy current 300 metres from the safe dry rock, bleeding from a third piece of missing flesh, and I was trying hard not to think of myself as food.'

If you've made the commitment to venture down to Tasmania, and if you've made the commitment to jump into the black, sharky waters, then you've only got one commitment left to make – but it's the big one. Taking off on a wave at Shipstern can be a real lottery. 'You can take off on an eight-footer on the outside ledge,' says Perrow, 'and it will be a 15-foot barrel on the inside. You just don't know what you're going to get.'

The abrupt force of Shipstern draws so much water off the reef, so quickly, that the wave face is often a facsimile of the craggy reef below. On a big swell with a low tide, and full sunlight for dramatic effect, the wave can look like a living Dali painting as it warps, twists and devours itself. But amidst the madness lies one of the biggest, throatiest barrels of all, and this is what many of the world's best surfers travel to Tassie to pit themselves against. Shipstern is open to everything the Southern Ocean can dish out, so swell is generally not a problem. But wind is: the secret is to look for a big 'H' parked over Tasmania on the weather map.

'The wave at the end of the world' might not be everyone's piece of cake, but for the hardcore surfer it's one stern test of internal fortitude, and offers a chance to be barrelled like you've never been barrelled before. And scoring the barrel of your life in this silent, ancient arena will turn a classic surfing moment into something undeniably cathartic.

shipstern bluff facts

location   South coast of Tasmania, around 45 km south of the capital, Hobart.

getting there   There's not enough space here to direct you in the detail required (turn left at the burnt stump, right at the dead wombat, etc., etc). Fly into Hobart, and purchase a good map.

the perfect day   Eight feet of southwest swell, northeast winds.

best months   February–May and September–November, the months either side of the southern-hemisphere winter.

boards   Something with a fair bit of volume to get you over the ledge and into the pit. Depending on swell, you'll start with a 6'4" and head up to something around 6'10". If the latter is skipping out, either get a ski and a tow board, or get the hell out of there while you still can.

essentials   Someone who knows what they're doing. There are cliffs to fall off, wrong tracks to take, wrong places to jump off.

accommodation   Shipstern isn't too far from the tourist hub of Port Arthur, or from Hobart itself, so there are plenty of options.

other waves   Tasmania has a ton of good surf, including a couple of world-class set-ups, although there's not much around Shipstern itself. Get a car and check it out.

soup bowls
barbados
kirk owers

Soup Bowls is quickly becoming one of this century's most lusted-after surf destinations. Located on the east coast of Barbados, this rotund, warm-water barrel flew under the radar for many a decade. Starring sections in two popular surf films – Campaign Two and Sipping Jetstreams – have it locked in the collective imagination as the Caribbean Backdoor. Regular visitor Kelly Slater says he's had one of the best surfs of his life at Soup Bowls. Now that's a recommendation.

Barbados, a former British colony, is the easternmost of the West Indies islands, which stretch from Venezuela north to Costa Rica. It is a place of luminous travel brochure clichés: white sandy beaches, swaying palm trees, calypso drum bands, gin-clear water, large-leafed jungle fringes, and beautiful tapering reef waves. In short, it looks like paradise. And with close to ideal year-round air and water temperatures, it feels like paradise too.

Surfing began here in the 60s when visiting Californians Butch Linden and Johnny Fain left their longboards behind for the local kids. The Bajans – descendants of West African slaves and their British overlords – took to the sport enthusiastically; competitions, amateur teams, surf shops and a local surfing association followed. Today surfing is a popular pursuit and local rippers such as Zed Layson and Mark Holder rule their home breaks.

183

Barbados has more than 30 known surf spots, but Soup Bowls is without doubt the alpha break. Its location on the east coast ensures plenty of swell year-round – it's estimated to be head-high or bigger 300 days a year, and is rarely flat. The downside to surfing the Atlantic coast is that it's often affected by onshore trade winds. Soup Bowls, however, barrels with such force that even a little onshore can't mess with it too much.

On a smaller day, Soup Bowls is a punchy, high-performance wave offering zippy barrels, banked cutback walls and trembling lips. At six feet it starts getting more serious – the barrels are powerful and fast, and the urchin-covered reef becomes a concern. During an eight-foot north swell, the Backdoor comparison becomes evident. The wave drains from take-off and, a clean entry requires supreme skill. Barrels are thick, warped and unpredictable. Often it'll shut down on the shallow inside reef.

Paradise it may well resemble, but a behind full of sea urchins is still a behind full of sea urchins. Plucking them out will take the shine off even the finest scenery. Kelly Slater enjoys the wave at size because it stretches his barrel-riding skills. The average surfer will be stoked to know that the heaving waves Slater rode during *Campaign II* are a rare event in Barbados; he waited a long time to surf it at that size, and those particularly heavy waves are not indicative of typical conditions at the break. This is the Caribbean, after all.

Barbados is a joy for most westerners to visit. While it has all the exotica of an island paradise it is also, oddly, British. English is the first language, place names are easy to pronounce, street signs make sense, cars drive on the left, and cricket is the national sport. It's a compact country with a pretty good road system. If the onshore picks up, you can be surfing in 30 minutes. Nothing is more than an hour away by car. The local surfers, if you are respectful, are laid back and hospitable.

Rumours tell of other world-class waves on Barbados, and a quick glance at a map suggests the nearby islands harbour equal potential. A base camp at Bathsheba, the town closest to Soup Bowls, could be the start of a memorable Caribbean surf adventure.

soup bowls facts

location   Near Bathsheba on the east coast of Barbados, Lesser Antilles islands, Caribbean Sea.

getting there   Fly to the Barbados capital, Bridgetown, which is also on the east coast.

the perfect day   Six-foot north swell, wide-open caverns all morning, dead calm. Light afternoon sea breeze and abating swell equal afternoon demolition session.

best months   Consistent swell (and onshore trades) all year round, but biggest and best October–March.

boards   A shortboard and one with a bit more length. Take several in case you snap a few.

essentials   Sunscreen, chilled attitude to everything.

accommodation   A good place to start looking is barbados.org/stay.

other waves   Plenty of known surf spots and some secret ones as well. The Caribbean side is offshore most of the year but usually receives smaller waves.

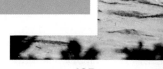

sunset beach
hawaii
sean doherty

'Sunset's not a surfing contest . . . it's a wave-catching contest.' In summing up the hi-cred pro tour event at Sunset Beach in this way, former winner Jake Paterson gives an insight into what one of Hawaii's most famous waves is all about – a real test of what you know about the ocean. Sunset is a wave that matters to real surfers.

The deepwater righthander holds special significance to the Hawaiians. Their ancestors were surfing out here over 800 years ago, and throughout the 60s and 70s, before Pipeline was being regularly challenged, Sunset was the wave on the North Shore. Since then it has gone in and out of fashion – if a surf break can do such a thing. Breaking 400 metres from shore, it's hard to tell what's really going on out there from shore, but once you're in the line-up, the place becomes pure theatre.

Surfing Sunset is a study in fluid dynamics. The size of several football fields, the line-up is so big you can literally get lost out here, and the energy that rumbles through is both diffuse and concentrated at the same time. The peaky nature of the break means that two guys can be sitting three metres apart when a set rolls through, and one will drop into the wave of his life while the other drops about nine metres to the ocean floor.

The reason for the trademark Sunset peak, and whole randomness of the line-up, is three long ridges of reef jutting out to sea behind the break. They split the incoming lines of swell and refract them into the giant lumbering peaks the break is famous for. There is really no right place to sit, but there are plenty of wrong ones.

The wave itself has three sections that all operate independently. Backyards is the furthest up the reef, with Sunset Point closer to the main break. Both are predominately righthanders and are popular on smaller swells. True Sunset is a very different proposition. It only starts to show when the swell is six to eight feet, but in the right conditions will take 15 feet-plus. The nature of the wave depends largely on the swell direction. When the swell's pure north, the peaks tend to run more down the point and be a touch more forgiving. When it's west, the peaks rear up from the deepwater behind the break and wrap dangerously into themselves as the wave steams through the inside. The ride is basically a big, majestic bottom turn, a couple of big-board speed turns, then a set-up of the infamous chew 'n' spew inside barrel section.

This is not a place to test out your new 5'8" fish, or your 720 McTwist rodeo clown. Sunset is strictly stern looks, knowing nods of the head, big boards and big turns. And due to the slow taper of the reef, for every foot longer your board is out here, you can sit another 20 metres out to sea. The result is that on mid-size days, the place is cluttered with guys sitting ridiculously far out on giant boards, picking off all the sets but not being able to do anything with them.

The sheer scope of Sunset means that it can be a dangerous place to surf when it gets size, and it's got half a dozen ways to hand you your tail on a plate. A hold-down here will often see you drilled so deep that the water literally goes black and you're forced to climb your legrope to the surface. You can wander too far up the reef toward the point and be caught inside in the section known as Boneyards. You can be swatted by a big west set that grows out of the channel with no warning. But maybe worst, and most spirit-sapping of all, is to lose your board in a big west swell and get caught in the whirlpool rip that flushes out through the channel, only to deposit you back in the line-up for you to do it all over again.

There's a reason they don't call the contest the Sunset Masters; it's because no surfer really ever can claim to have mastered it.

sunset beach facts

location   Oahu's North Shore, Hawaii.

getting there   Fly into Honolulu. A one-hour drive will get you to the North Shore.

the perfect day   Ten feet of northwest swell, a light easterly trade wind, late January with little crowd.

best months   October to March, with post-Christmas your best bet to beat the madding crowd.

boards   Time to break out the big boards, boys. If it's real Sunset, the smallest board you'll contemplate riding will be a 6'6" to a 6'8". If it gets serious, you could be on something 8'0" and up.

essentials   Some solid surf fitness, an ability to deal with a long hold-down, a willingness to learn some lessons from the ocean, and a pushbike to get around on.

accommodation   Ultra-busy with exorbitant tariffs in November and December. Book something on the internet for only the first week, then find something that'll suit you better. Most North Shore pilgrims stay with the same local family, year after year.

other waves   The 11-km North Shore has more waves than you could ever know what to do with. Pipe, Sunset and Waimea are just the ones you've heard about.

tamarin bay
mauritius
sean doherty

'Santosha isn't really a particular place, it's a word that has a meaning . . . It's a state of mind, actually, a state of being, of living . . . To me It seems a forgotten state of happiness and peace.' When *The Forgotten Island of Santosha* was first published in 1974, Larry Yates' seminal account of his visit to the magical isle of Mauritius and its magical lefthander fuelled the wanderlust of surfers, opening their eyes to worlds beyond their local beach break. Quixotic travellers were soon hitting the road with a board under one arm and barely two coins to rub together, looking for their own slice of surfing nirvana. 'Santosha' became a metaphor for the escapism that was opening up huge tracts of the surfable planet. It was little surprise that Lagundri was discovered the following year, Grajagan three years later, and Tavarua not long after that.

It's easy to imagine how Mauritius seduced the first guys to venture there – and why they tried so hard to keep it from the ravages of their fellow surferkind. An isolated volcanic rook roughly halfway between Africa and Asia, the place has been a melting pot of cultures for centuries, and for an island roughly 50 kilometres square, it has been splashed with more history per hectare than anywhere outside Europe. From spice traders to pirates, from sugar-cane slaves to French colonialists, Mauritius has long been a sanctuary for continental refugees, many of whom never left. The island's population today is a unique mix of Creole, Indians, Chinese and French, and the Hindu majority adds a real touch of the exotic.

Coming down from the psychedelic Santosha high and dealing with the reality of Tamarin today can, though, be a real bummer. The wave is still there, but the dream has largely gone the way of the dodo, the flightless native bird that was clubbed into extinction soon after man first set foot on the island in the 16th century. On its day Cap Dal – as the lefthander at Tamarin Bay is known to locals – is an epic barrel running down a sharp and shallow coral reef. The swells that wrap into Jeffrey's Bay in South Africa will do likewise at Tamarin two days later. However, Tamarin's sheltered position (it basically faces northwest) means that it needs a lot of this swell before it starts firing. Visiting surfers have chewed the ears off their friends at home with horror tales of waiting three weeks at Tamarin without seeing a surfable swell, and that's during peak season. If you're travelling to Tamarin looking for surf, bring a set of cards.

The inconsistent nature of the break has also contributed to the reputation the place has for localism. What Larry Yates would make of the White Shorts we can only guess. The Indian Ocean's equivalent of the Hawaiian Black Shorts, these mainly ex-pat surfers have developed a gnarly reputation for making life uncomfortable for visiting surfers, particularly at Tamarin. And while the biped locals can be heavy on blow-in surfers, the locals in grey suits can be even heavier. Mauritius is home to a large shark population, and the long paddles out to the fringing reefs are often nervous-making. The danger of having a chunk taken out of you varies wildly, depending on whom you talk to – a hotel owner will tell you they're all friendly little reef sharks, a local surfer will tell you the surf is patrolled by the world's biggest tigers.

The Santosha of the 70s may have gone a bit Club Med, and the empty waves Larry Yates found at Tamarin have become a little busier, but Mauritius still has a rare quality that's worth at least a week's stickybeak on your way to J-Bay.

tamarin bay facts

location   The west coast of Mauritius, which lies west of Madagascar in the Indian Ocean.

getting there   Due to the fact it's become a high-demand tourist destination, there are plenty of flights to Mauritius; it's even got its own airline.

the perfect day   Four–six feet of southwest swell, light easterly winds, and enough tide to keep you off the reef.

best months   April–September.

boards   Pack up as if you're heading to Indonesia. A couple of shortboard options and something up around 6'6" in case you hit the jackpot and the place cops a swell.

essentials   Sunscreen, a good medical kit, and a willingness to travel all the way to Mauritius knowing you may not even get to paddle out at Tamarin Bay.

accommodation   While much of it is pitched at rich French tourists, there are still enough budget *pensions* to cater for the scumbag surfer.

other waves   Check out Black Rock on the other side of the bay, and there are several other waves on the south and west coasts of the island.

teahupoo
tahiti
sean doherty

It's strange to think that only a decade ago the surfing world had never heard of Teahupoo. The world's most infamous wave had sat unchallenged in this remote, pre-historic corner of the South Pacific since Year Dot, waiting for someone with more balls than brains to surf it. In the 10 years since its blanket exposure, surfers (albeit fishing in a small pool) have run out of adjectives to describe it. 'Chopes', as Teahupoo is also known, is now regarded as the most savage wave in the world. From the 50 waves to surf before you die, this is the one most likely be the actual cause of your death.

When the first images of Teahupoo passed across the lightbox at *Tracks* magazine back in 1998, we thought we were looking at something from Mars. Three storeys high, electric blue and airbrushed smooth, they looked like pure science-fiction. It wasn't just the size of the waves, however, it was the pure elemental aggro in each one that stunned us. They were like horizontal tornadoes. The waves' lips were thicker than the waves themselves were high, and they seemingly defied physics by breaking below sea level. We, like the first Tahitians who paddled out there in the 80s, were wondering how in hell this place could actually be surfed.

The ancient Tahitians knew of the place's potential for dismemberment and named it Teahupoo, which roughly translates to 'scraped head'. Millennia of freshwater runoff carved a pass through Tahiti's fringing coral reef, and Teahupoo sits at the southern entrance of the pass, nearly a kilometre out to sea, facing into the vastness of the South Pacific. The ferocity of the wave owes much to the topography of the ocean floor that skirts the break. As abruptly as the volcanic mountains rise behind the nearby village, the ocean floor drops away behind the wave. With no continental shelf, the first landfall that sub-Antarctic swells make after travelling 10 000 kilometres is a hard-packed, waist-deep horse-shoe of razor-sharp coral. Welcome to Teahupoo.

The wave has killed before, and is very likely to kill again. In 2000 local surfer Briece Taoroa lost his life after being caught inside by a 12-foot set, dragged over the falls before landing head-first on the reef. Some of the world's best surfers, due here for the world tour contest in May each year, have been known to contract 'Teahupoo Fever' – a mystery recurrence of an old injury which conveniently flares

The first landfall that sub-Antarctic swells make is a hard-packed, waist-deep horseshoe of razor-sharp coral. Welcome to Teahupoo.

up just before they are to board the plane for Tahiti. This wave is a scary piece of work, and in recent years it has become a tow-surfing Colosseum, where an assortment of local and visiting hellmen have collaborated to redefine the term 'surfable'.

The fishing village of Teahupoo belies the hype surrounding the aquatic monster offshore. It is literally the end of the road, as beyond Teahupoo the mountains become too steep to put a road through. The dogs outnumber the surf stars, and the place is serviced by half a supermarket and a couple of palm-thatched shacks. Unless you enjoy half-hour-long paddles, you'll need to hire a boat and a driver, as almost all the area's waves break on the outer reefs;

and be warned, the exchange rate for the Tahitian franc makes the wave itself look like a neutered pussycat. On the bright side, the locals are amongst the friendliest, most laid-back people on Earth.

So, as a travelling surfer, why would you ever want to visit Teahupoo? Two reasons. The first is the fact that, up to six feet (which is 95 per cent of the year), the wave really is the Tahitian dream – a perfect, sectionless, tropical barrel. This, however, is where the dream ends, because above this size it becomes the work of the Devil himself. This leads to the second reason you should visit the place. To observe (from the safety of the channel) this place at 12 feet is to know what a wave can do. There is no more brutal, beautiful spectacle in the surfing cosmos, and it is worth being there if only to watch it.

teahupoo facts

location Havae Pass, Teahupoo, on the south coast of Tahiti Iti in French Polynesia.

getting there Fly into the capital, Papeete, on the north coast, from where it's a one-hour drive.

the perfect day Eight feet of southwest swell, mid-morning trade winds, and just a handful of Tahitian locals for company.

best months April–August, although the southwest swells often keep arriving as late as December.

boards For small days a shortboard will do. At four–eight feet you'll need something between 6'4" and 6'8" with a bit of volume in it (to paddle into the wave). Bring two more boards than you think you'll need, as you're very likely to snap at least one.

essentials A (very) good medical kit, some basic French or Tahitian, a good chunk of your life savings, a willingness to scare yourself witless.

accommodation There are several local *pensions* with affordable beds. For something five-star and poolside, head back toward Papeete.

other waves There are several quality reef breaks in the area, all of which require either a boat ride or a marathon paddle – and none of which the locals will be too keen to tell you about.

the island
new zealand
derek morrison

Few waves in New Zealand carry the level of reverence that the Island does. It's a wave that defines pecking orders, rewards the men and slams the hesitant. Even on big, clean days with lines stacked to eternity, the line-up is collectively apprehensive. It's a wave of consequence and is sufficiently removed from Gisborne, the nearest town, to make any surfer feel isolated, vulnerable and insignificant.

Gisborne has been considered one of New Zealand's prime surfing regions ever since local hellman Kevin Pritchard and a bunch of his mates plucked up the courage to surf Makorori Point in the early 1960s. Word got out, and shortly afterwards travelling Aussies and Americans began to swarm through the area, adding colour to the emerging surf culture in New Zealand with music, ideas and psychedelica. Gisborne was the vanguard of surf culture: Jimi Hendrix, The Doors and all the late-60s music icons entered the country through this wide-eyed port. Even Malibu's surfing rogue, Mickey Dora, managed to escape international authorities by hiding out (surfing his brains out) in Gisborne during this opulent surf era.

It wasn't until many years later that the Island first got surfed in all its glory. Its belated discovery sprang partly from its relative remoteness: to get to the line-up, you have to paddle nearly a kilometre from Sponge Bay to Tuamotu Island, then run 150 metres across the island to where you can paddle out. At low tide you can walk the whole distance over slippery rocks – a trek that's guaranteed to skin at least a couple of toes. Locals often take boats out to the Island to maximise energy expenditure on the wave itself, rather than on getting there. Either way, a session here requires a bit more time and organisation than your average reef break. The cruel twist is that you can't actually see the wave from the car park at Sponge Bay. It's a leap of faith for the unwise, but locals have the ideal wind and swell directions imprinted on their minds at birth so there is scarcely a solitary moment out there when the break is in its prime.

One kilometre down the road is Wainui Beach, home of the equally fabled Stock Route, Pines and Whales – quality beach breaks that are renowned for producing Puerto Escondido-esque barrels. The Island itself is an Indo-like left reef break that grinds down the southwestern side of Tuamotu. It has distinct outside and inside sections, but it is the outside's Bowl that has given this place its lofty status. Refracting swell lines rise out of deep water onto the reef in a concave shape that is doubly distorted by the water sucking off the reef itself. It's a heavy take-off that leads straight into the equally serious Bowl section. There have been many sessions here punctuated by a parade of surfers picking their way back through the rocks with a piece of board in each hand. After the Bowl, the left peels beautifully to the inside, where the shallow reef tends to create very fast, very sucky, rifling barrels.

On days over six feet, the righthand reef break known as Outside Island begins to work. It operates more like an offshore bombie and produces the type of waves that Mark Sutherland used to draw in his Gonad Man comic strip. Like the Island it's a break of consequence, though far less consistent, and getting a wave at Outside Island is something you will never, ever forget – you may even have a souvenir scar to remember it by.

the island facts

location   Across from Sponge Bay, 5 km east of Gisborne on the east coast of New Zealand's North Island.

getting there   You can fly to Auckland, Hamilton or Palmerston North. There are regular flights to Gisborne from Auckland. Expect at least a five-hour drive from Hamilton and Palmerston North, seven from Auckland.

the perfect day   Eight-foot southerly groundswell, combined with a superlight northerly wind.

best months   March through to November will see the busiest groundswell traffic from the Southern Ocean. The northerly and westerly airstreams are more predictable November–June.

boards   On days over four feet, a smallish gun. If you want manoeuvrability with a bigger tail, then a drivey bottom shape or fins will help. At less than four feet you can get away with a fast-accelerating beach-break shape. More volume will be a boon on that long, long paddle back!

essentials   For winter you'll need a 4/3 steamer, and booties wouldn't go astray. In summer a 2/3 springy will do, but the water can be on the cooler side even then.

accommodation   You have an abundance of options, from farmstays to first-class executive suites. Check out www.gisborne.co.nz for links to help you in your search. A place at Wainui Beach will place you in walking distance of the surf.

other waves   Nearby Makorori Point is a very long, occasionally grunty right point that's worth a look. It's also worth exploring the East Cape to the north, and Mahia Peninsula an hour south.

the superbank
australia
sean doherty

It's one of the great wonders of the surfing world, but Mother Nature can only take half the credit for Queensland's Superbank. While man has utterly extinguished the natural beauty of the Gold Coast, it is the ultimate irony that he's been able to create a thing of true beauty – even if it was by mistake. It seems that in the home of the cheeseball tourist theme park, they've even made one for surfers.

In 2001, the Gold Coast council fired up the pumps to start dredging the mouth of the Tweed River, making it safer for fishing boats to put to sea. The sand was to be pumped to the northern side of the river mouth, behind Snapper Rocks, whence it would continue its natural drift north up the Queensland coast. When the dredge contractor pushed the button on that morning, he had no idea he would soon become a cult hero for surfers around the world.

Within weeks the local surfers began to notice the change. The adjacent (yet independent) point breaks of Snapper Rocks and Greenmount were being cemented together by a blanket of sand. A few months later the magic dust had spread out into the bay, the high-tide line was 150 metres further out, and the new wave was even linking up with Kirra, two kilometres away. It was Frankenstein's monster, only much, much prettier – it was the Superbank coming to life. Gold Coast surfers couldn't believe what they were seeing. Guys were scoring the waves of their lives. Twenty-second tubes were clocked; one local surfer, Damon Harvey, rode a wave from Snapper Rocks all the way through to Little Groyne at Kirra. And it wasn't just that the wave was long – it barrelled, walled, spat and slithered all the way. The thing was damn-near flawless, whichever way you looked at it.

The wave begins behind the rock at Snapper – Satan's washing machine. The heaviest section of the whole wave, it's the backwash off Snapper's rocks that makes the take-off here so sketchy, and it's here that the local guys rule. If you survive this below-sea-level barrel section – which the locals have an uncanny knack of doing – the next kilometre or two is all yours (or, more to the point, theirs). Beyond this, the nature of the wave itself fluctuates according to the state of the sand. As a rule, the wave barrels through Little Marley, backs off slightly heading into Greenmount, then goes to the races through Coolangatta into Kirra. But don't worry so much about what the wave's going to do, just worry about getting one.

Cue the circus music, because the best sandbank in the world was never going to remain a secret for very long. Flawless would soon become lawless. The perfect nature of the wave means that it rarely sections off, so, in theory, a five-wave set can be ridden by five guys for as long as they want. With another 500 guys in the water waiting their turn . . . well, you crunch the numbers. The only way to get a wave is to either take off behind the rock, hope the guy on the wave chokes and falls, or simply burn him. Sadly, the latter scenario is all too

The new wave was even linking up with Kirra, two kilometres away. It was Frankenstein's monster, only much, much prettier – it was the Superbank coming to life.

common out here, and the place occasionally degenerates into a post-apocalyptic war zone. From 70-year-olds to seven-year-olds, from Brazilians to the British, from weekend warriors to world champs, they're all thrown together out there, battling each other for their little slice of the legend.

But what man can build, nature can wipe away in a heartbeat, and you always get the feeling there's something impermanent about the Superbank. It will only exist as long as the pumps keep pumping. The bank's short existence has coincided with one of the quietest meteorological periods in modern history, and the place hasn't yet experienced a direct hit from an overdue tropical cyclone. Maybe Huey, seeing that the place is conjuring up the dark side of the surfing spirit, will do a Sodom and Gomorrah on the Superbank and wash away all trace of it.

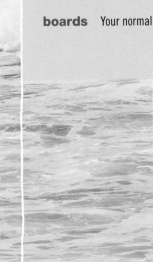

the superbank facts

location The Gold Coast, on the southern coast of Queensland, about 100 km south of the state capital, Brisbane.

getting there Fly to Coolangatta, which is five minutes away.

the perfect day Four feet of easterly swell courtesy of a cyclone south of New Caledonia, light southwesterly wind.

best months February through to August, as the cyclone swells from the north give way to powerful winter southerlies.

boards Your normal shortboard will be fine.

essentials Patience: each surf out here will either be close to the best of your life or the worst, never anything in between. You also need to be pretty fit, as the rip running down the point is ferocious and you'll be paddling the entire time.

accommodation Being a tourist town, there are plenty of units.

other waves If you ride one of these things long enough you'll eventually be surfing through Kirra, one of the world's most famous waves. Burleigh Heads is 20 minutes north and Lennox Head 40 minutes south.

thurso east
scotland
d.c. green

Thurso East is fickle, faraway and frosty – no surprise for a wave located so far north it's actually inside the Arctic Circle. But when big lows cavort off Iceland or the North Pole, the pride of the Scottish Highlands mutates into the northern hemisphere's Lagundri Bay: a flawless righthand reef with power and pits. Says pioneer Pat Keiran: 'Thurso never closes out. I've seen it at 20 feet, with the same shape as at six.'

In 1978, Kiwi Bob Treeby became the first surfer to pull into Thurso's dark, almond eyes. Things haven't changed much since. Of five million Scots (one-twelfth of Britain), only 500 are surfers and about 10 of these live in the cobble-stoned town of Thurso. Thurso's surf industry could well be the most undeveloped of any similar-sized town in the western world; even the one surf shop is boarded up. 'It's not exactly Baywatch,' comments Pat Keiran.

Not that Thurso is a secret spot. The wave has hosted the European, British and Scottish surf titles, the World Surf Kayak championships (!) and the inaugural O'Neill Highland Open World Qualifying Series 5-star in 2006, won in throaty kegs by Russell Winter. There are good reasons why this Scottish gem isn't overrun. The water temperature can plunge as low as 4°C, at which wax turns to granite and testicles migrate to throats. One local's snap-frozen wetsuit shattered when he snatched it from the line. In spring, chunks of ice – some the size of car roofs – flush through the peat-stained line-up seeking unwary luxury liners and thruster fins.

Summer has a different hazard: sleep deprivation. You can still be surfing at 11 at night, slug down a few pints and get back in the water at 2 a.m. Unfortunately, summer is also mostly flat. However, the biggest put-off is the nearby Dounreay nuclear facility, responsible for the odd lethal radioactive particle popping up on local beaches. Oh, and though the locals aren't numerous, they're definitely hardcore. Rumbles Andy Bain, 15-plus tonnes and tatt-forearmed: 'I can be your best friend or your worst nightmare. There's only one road out of town, and it's a long way home.' For those who show respect, Thurso's population is a surprisingly tolerant, even cosmopolitan mix. Backpackers arrive daily to ferry north to the Orkneys. German scientists wave. Yet there's also an undertone of olde-world conservatism. Andy Bain: 'If you come back from overseas wearing surf clothes, people tend to brand you a bit of a weird nut.'

If Cornwall is the beer-swollen heart of British surfing, Scotland is the hairy gonads beneath the kilt: extreme in latitude, landscape, climate and characters. To score Thurso, patience is a must. I holed up through several days of sleet and snow just to score one surfable day shadowed by the stone ruins of Lord Thurso's manor. By the end of my second session, I was gibbering with hypothermia. Next day, I could barely move as my muscles were so stiff from shaking, and my brain-cell count has never been the same since. Worth it? Um, what?

thurso east facts

location   Far north coast of Scotland, between John O'Groats and Tongue.

getting there   A 15-hour drive from London to the top of Scotland. The nearest airport is at Inverness, around 180 km away.

the perfect day   Midwinter, midweek, uncrowded, light offshore, six–eight feet. Waves pump all day. Pity the day lasts barely five hours!

best months   October–March (late autumn to spring)

boards   Standard board through to a gun, as the reef packs punch and can get big. Boards with more volume are handy, to float higher above the icy water.

essentials   6/5 steamer, hood, booties, gloves, earplugs, thermal underwear, sense of humour, high pain and whisky thresholds.

accommodation   Thurso and the harbour town of Scrabster have pubs and motels.

other waves   Nearby is the poetically named Shit Pipe. The north coast of Scotland is dotted with beaches, reefs and offshore islands, mostly undocumented.

uluwatu
bali
sean doherty

Almost 1000 years ago a whole village of Balinese chose to throw themselves off the cliffs at Uluwatu rather than succumb to the invading Javanese. Almost 40 years ago, western surfers started throwing themselves off the cliff in order to escape nine-to-five employment.

A small Hindu island within a massive Muslim nation, Bali has always possessed a unique spirit that has intoxicated surfers since the early 1970s. The discovery of surf in Bali – more particularly, Uluwatu – is the stuff of legend, as it was all documented in surfing's most timeless and referenced film, *Morning of the Earth*.

Film-maker Albe Falzon arrived in Bali in late 1970 with surfers Rusty Miller and 15-year-old schoolboy Steve Cooney in tow, and little idea what to expect. When Albe, with a silent, knowing smile, returned one afternoon from a reconnoitring mission up the Bukit Peninsula, Steve Cooney knew Albe had found something more than his inner glow.

'The road from Kuta to the Monkey Temple was a winding mess of potholes, barely wide enough for two bemos to pass each other,' recalls Steve. 'The Balinese were very wary of Uluwatu and regarded it as an evil place to be treated very carefully. When they realised we were actually going to go out in the water they seemed to become nervous and a little suspicious of our intentions.

'As I turned to take the first wave of the session everything seemed to go into slow motion. One of the most enjoyable aspects of Uluwatu at that time was the abundance of sea life. At high tide the dugongs would come over the reef with their calves and loll about in the shallows, going back outside the reef as the tide dropped. When we were surfing at low tide they would surface near us and let us know they were around. They were there the whole time and seemed as interested in us as we were in them. There were turtles, reef snakes, heaps of fish, sea birds and sea snakes. We never felt as if we were on our own in the water.'

It wasn't long before Australian surfers began to discover the place *en masse*. They soon realised that while Uluwatu had a magic quality, the whole island was crawling with world-class set-ups. From Uluwatu down the Bukit Peninsula through Padang, Impossibles, Bingin, Dreamland and Balangan, it is a rare convergence of epic lefthand reefs. Ulus is furthest up the peninsula, and as such draws in the most swell; the line-up has several moods that show their faces accordingly, depending on swell and tide. The Temples section can handle 15 feet, as will Outside Corner, but real Uluwatu materialises on smaller swells, six–eight feet, running down the inside reef. The Peak is the take-off spot on high tide, while at low tide it moves down 100 metres to the Racetrack. On a clean swell the sections will link up and you can backdoor barrel sections for a couple of hundred metres over the sharp coral reef.

> **The only route in and out of the break is through the legendary cave, a quasi-religious experience until you have to paddle back through it on a high tide and big swell.**

The only route in and out of the break at Uluwatu is through the legendary cave, a quasi-religious experience until you have to paddle back through it on a high tide and big swell. If you overshoot, you will

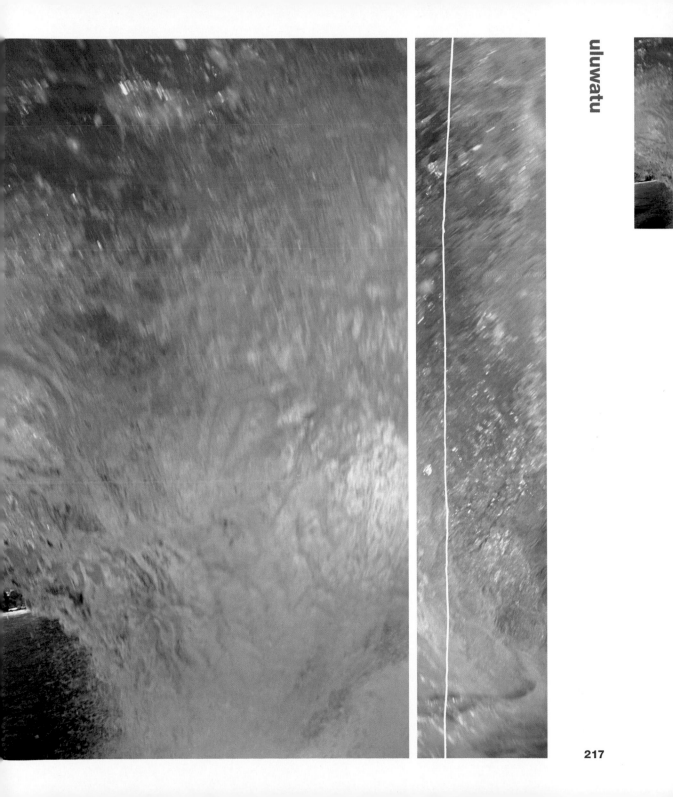

find little quasi-religious about being dragged along the dagger-like cliffs for more than a kilometre, all the way down to Padang.

Unfortunately, what was once an intensely spiritual journey up the Bukit has become soulless to many travellers today. The dirt track out to Ulus is now a bitumen highway, and the friendly monkeys the *Morning of the Earth* crew encountered at the Ulu temple have now acquired the skill of stealing your peanuts with one hand while pilfering your wallet with the other.

Even after the 2002 and 2004 bombings, Bali continues to attract a cosmopolitan army of surfers from around the globe. Australians, Brazilians, Japanese and Europeans all flock to the place, seduced by its incredible surf, cheap living, and party vibe. But while the Balinese dream may have been tarnished, the endearing spirit of the Balinese people remains an unwavering constant. The number of filed-tooth smiles you encounter as you walk down the Uluwatu track will convince you that all is still *bagus* in Bali.

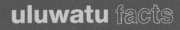

location   Bukit Peninsula, south of Denpasar in Bali, Indonesia.

getting there   Fly into Denpasar, and then it's bemo (the local taxi) all the way to Uluwatu. If you fancy becoming a statistic, you can join the thousands of temporary humans riding scooters.

the perfect day   Six–eight feet of southwest swell, light easterly trades, high tide.

best months   April–September, the local dry season.

boards   A couple of inches longer than your standard shortboard – this is a powerful reef break, after all. If it gets above eight feet, you're going to need 6'8"-plus, as you'll be doing a lot of paddling.

essentials   Manners, and a willingness to absorb the vibe of the place. Respect the place and the people, and you'll get infinitely more from your trip. And don't take green boardies, they're considered bad luck.

accommodation   Plenty of it and it's cheap.

other waves   Down the peninsula you've got Padang Padang (undoubtedly a better wave than Ulus, just less consistent), Impossibles, Bingin, Dreamland and Balangan. Around the eastern side of the island the perfect lefts turn into perfect right – Sanur, Keramas. Arguably the world's two best lefthanders, G-Land and Desert Point, are both within a short sail.

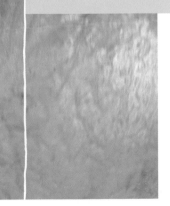

waimea bay
hawaii
sean doherty

For decades, Waimea Bay has possessed a sacred aura for surfers. Ever since the Duke was in short pants, big-wave surfing began – and ended – with 'the Bay'. But it's Waimea's spiritual connection to the ancient Hawaiians that makes paddling out here as much a sublime experience as a test of internal fortitude.

The Hawaiians lived in the Valley of the Priests behind Waimea Bay for more than 1000 years, and the ruins of two ancient stone temples (*heiaus*) are eerie reminders of a time long before Kam Highway traffic jams. And while just down the road Pipeline is dominated by young surfers with fire in their bellies, the take-off zone at Waimea is populated with Hawaiian surfing royalty – legendary names like Aikau, Ho, and Kinimaka – all riding impossibly long boards. It's almost as if the ghosts of the early kings have paddled out from the valley to take their place in the line-up.

As you catch your first glimpse of the bay, it's often hard to reconcile what you're seeing with the big-wave colossus you've grown up hearing about. It is flat on most days of the year, and one of the island's most popular family beaches. Carved out by freshwater flows over tens of thousands of years, the spoon-shaped bay, nearly a kilometre across, is lined by black volcanic boulders at its northern end, while at its western corner is an erratic scattering of rock formations, one of which is a favourite with the local *keikis* (kids) who jump off it into the calm ocean.

Add 20 feet of swell, however, and the place is unrecognisable – a churning, seething mass of whitewater with a booming righthand peak off the northern point. Unlike most of Oahu's north shore, there are no outside reefs off Waimea to refract or subdue the swell energy, and when it's on it seems as if the entire North Pacific is pouring into the bay. The wave itself is pretty well just a drop, rearing up as it does out of deep water onto a flat lava shelf. There is only one way to deal with the peak at Waimea – pick your wave, put your head down, and paddle like there's no tomorrow. Hesitate, and that might just be the case. There's a good chance, however, that your Waimea pilgrimage may only get you as far as the high-tide line. Requiring a big, clean swell before the wave even starts to show itself, there are only a handful of 'Bay days' every year. The fact that the annual Eddie Aikau Big Wave Memorial contest has only run seven times in 20 years is testament to the fact that classic Waimea requires a rare alignment of the elements. Many surfers wait months for a day that never comes.

There is only one way to deal with the peak at Waimea – pick your wave, put your head down, and paddle like there's no tomorrow.

If you do happen to luck on a swell, then there's the small matter of actually surfing it. The volume of water moving in and out of the bay is truly frightening, and you need a fair set of figs – and a fair belief in your own surfing aptitude – to even contemplate paddling out. And while you may not have the bottle to paddle out, just sitting on the rocks watching the day unfold will often be enough sensory bombardment for you to feel inclined to cross Waimea off your list anyway.

The bay has taken some lives,

most recently in December 1995 when the young Californian surfer Donnie Solomon split a set wave with Kelly Slater and Ross Clarke-Jones, only to be caught inside soon after by a giant close-out set. His lifeless body was dragged up onto the beach soon after. But just as the stones of the *heiaus* echo the cries of an ancient time, the wave at Waimea Bay is a relic of an era of surfing that has largely been left behind. The advent of tow-surfing in the late 90s opened up large tracts of bigger, better surf right around the world. But while Waimea has ceased to be a performance surfing arena, it remains – and will so for the next 1000 years – an important link to surfing's roots.

waimea bay facts

location   North shore of the island of Oahu, Hawaii.

getting there   Fly into Honolulu, from where it's a 45-minute drive north.

the perfect day   Twenty feet of clean, long northwest swell, with light easterly trade winds.

best months   November–March, although the later in the season you leave it the less company you'll have on the peak.

boards   Time to dust off the big boys. Your smallest will need to clock in around 8'0", but most serious Waimea guys paddle out on boards closer to 10'0".

essentials   If you're serious about paddling out here, you'll want to devote the best part of the previous decade to the goal. Physically, mentally, spiritually — you need to be well prepared. A local buddy to guide you around the line-up will also be handy.

accommodation   Waimea has some of the more affordable options on the North Shore. If you're accustomed to something more ritzy, stay in Honolulu and drive out from there.

other waves   Five minutes down the road you'll find more surf than you know what to do with.

D.C. GREEN   D.C. Green has been one of Australia's leading surf writers for two decades. His first gig was writing the sacrilegious and seminal 'Lash Clone' columns in the pages of *Tracks*. D.C. takes the Gonzo approach to his work, which has allowed him to write some profound and touching stories no other surf journalist would have been able to extract from the ether. His intimate knowledge of the reef at One Palm Point was gained while drydocked there in 2002. Living on the New South Wales south coast, D.C. has recently embarked on a career writing books for children.

MATT GRIGGS   Matt Griggs grew up around the reefs of his native Cronulla, south of Sydney, and he is unlikely to live anywhere else. A former pro surfer himself, Matt took up surf journalism in 2001, becoming staff writer with *Tracks* magazine. Soon after, he penned *The Surfers*, a collection of short bios on the world's best wave-riders. Often referring to himself in the third person as 'Doctor Yes', in 2004 Matt became Pit Boss with the Rip Curl surf team, travelling the world coaching and mentoring some of the world's best surfers.

CRAIG JARVIS   Craig Jarvis lives near Durban in South Africa, but has spent a good portion of his existence chasing surf all over the planet. His piece here on Bundoran Peak fails to mention that he came to grief on the aforementioned reef, almost tearing himself a new orifice in the process. A larger-than-life character, he is a master storyteller, a skill which only improves with every beer. A former editor of South Africa's *Zig Zag* surfing magazine, he currently writes freelance.

BEN MONDY   Ben Mondy is a freelance writer, and wandering editor for *Tracks* magazine. He contributes regularly to *Surfer Magazine* in the US, and to several surfing and sports titles throughout Europe. Ben was raised in the maligned lefts of his native Redhead Beach, on the central New South Wales coast, and his surfing style bares an uncanny resemblance to that of former female world champ, Pam Burridge. Ben currently resides in sunny downtown London, where classic point breaks are few, but his naturally pale skin allows him to blend in with the natives.

DEREK MORRISON   Derek grew up on the North Island of New Zealand, where his early grommethood was spent chasing sheep on horseback. Once he got his driving licence, and realised that sheep were tastier than they were cute, the long lefts of Raglan began calling. He took a job with *New Zealand Surfing* magazine in 1998, and has spent the past nine years editing and contributing to various action-sports mags in both Australia and New Zealand. He currently calls Dee Why (on Sydney's northern beaches) home, where he lives with his wife Rachael and daughter Taya.

KIRK OWERS   Kirk grew up at Dudley Beach, just down the road from Ben Mondy. But while Ben had the long sandy lefts of Redhead to groom his surfing style on, Kirk had the once-a-year treacherous barrels of Dudley Point to contend with. He is a freelance surf and travel writer, and can often been seen sporting a thick and unkempt beard which betrays his green leanings. When he's not cavorting around the world on sponsored travel junkets, he can be found at his home on the New South Wales mid-north coast with his girl Helena and son Marley.

DAVE SPARKES   Dave Sparkes grew up in The Valley – as Bondi is known to the locals. From an early age he began devising ways to make a living out of surfing. Once he realised no one was going to pay him to actually go surfing, he embarked on a career writing about and photographing it. Today he is one of Australia's leading, true surfing photojournalists. He also holds the dubious, but fortuitous, distinction of being the only contributor to this book to have survived a full-blown shark attack, when a very large great white mistook him for a strangely proportioned fur seal early in 2007.

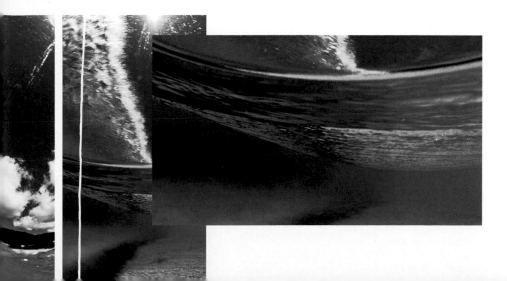

photo credits

Anchor Point
Bernard Testemale

Angourie
Slikpix

Arugam Bay
Anders

Bells Beach
Steve Ryan

Black Rock
Paul Gleeson

Burleigh
MTVz

Bundoran Peak
Roger Sharp

Cave Rock
Pablo Ponzone

Chicama
Jon Frank

Cloud Nine
John Callahan

Cloudbreak
Nathan Smith

Coxos
Bernard Testemale

Desert Point
Yazzy

Gnaraloo
Nathan Smith

Grajagan
Shorty

Haapiti
Jason Murray

Honolua Bay
Sean Davey

Hossegor
Bernard Testemale

Jeffrey's Bay
Garth Robinson

Joaquina
Luiz Blanco

Kirra
Nathan Smith

La Jolla
Dave Sparkes

Lagundri
Dave Sparkes

Lance's Right
Pete Frieden

Lennox Head
Andrew Christie

Macaronis
Nathan Smith

Margaret River
Jamie Scott

Mundaka
Tim Jones

Nihiwatu
Shorty

One Palm Point
Jason Childs

Pasta Point
Steve Robertson

Piha Bar
CPL

Pipeline
Shorty

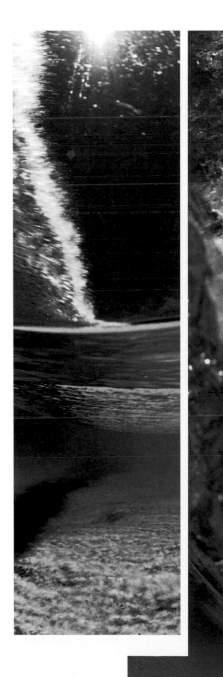

VIKING

Published by the Penguin Group
Penguin Group (Australia)
250 Camberwell Road, Camberwell, Victoria 3124, Australia
(a division of Pearson Australia Group Pty Ltd)
Penguin Group (USA) Inc.
375 Hudson Street, New York, New York 10014, USA
Penguin Group (Canada)
90 Eglinton Avenue East, Suite 700, Toronto, Canada ON M4P 2Y3
(a division of Pearson Penguin Canada Inc.)
Penguin Books Ltd
80 Strand, London WC2R 0RL England
Penguin Ireland
25 St Stephen's Green, Dublin 2, Ireland
(a division of Penguin Books Ltd)
Penguin Books India Pvt Ltd
11 Community Centre, Panchsheel Park, New Delhi – 110 017, India
Penguin Group (NZ)
67 Apollo Drive, Rosedale, North Shore 0632, New Zealand
(a division of Pearson New Zealand Ltd)
Penguin Books (South Africa) (Pty) Ltd
24 Sturdee Avenue, Rosebank, Johannesburg 2196, South Africa

Penguin Books Ltd, Registered Offices: 80 Strand, London, WC2R 0RL, England

First published by Penguin Group (Australia), 2007

10 9 8 7 6 5 4 3

Text copyright © Penguin Group (Australia), 2007
Photographs copyright © individual photographers

Cover and text design by Elizabeth Theodosiadis & Nicholas McGuire © Penguin Group (Australia)
Cover photograph of Lance's Right, Indonesia, by Pete Frieden
Typeset in Nimbus Sans Novus and DisEngage by Post Pre-press Group, Brisbane, Queensland
Scanning and separations by Splitting Image P/L, Clayton, Victoria
Printed and bound in China by Imago Productions

Cataloguing information for this book is available from the National Library of Australia

ISBN 978 0 670 07085 5

penguin.com.au